TALES
OF THE
DERVISHES

IDRIES SHAH

TALES
OF THE
DERVISHES

Teaching-stories of the Sufi
Masters over the past thousand years

Selected from the Sufi classics, from oral
tradition, from unpublished manuscripts and
schools of Sufi teaching in many countries

A Dutton  *Paperback*

E. P. DUTTON & CO., INC., NEW YORK

Library of Congress Catalog Card Number: 68-59638

SBN 0-525-47262-2

CONTENTS

TO MY TEACHERS

WHO TOOK WHAT WAS GIVEN
WHO GAVE WHAT COULD NOT BE TAKEN

Preface

This book contains stories from the teachings of Sufi masters and schools, recorded during the past thousand years.

The material has been collected from Persian, Arabic, Turkish and other classics; from traditional teaching-story collections, and from oral sources which include contemporary Sufi teaching centres.

It therefore represents 'work material' in current use as well as significant quotations from literature which has inspired some of the greatest Sufis of the past.

Teaching material used by Sufis has always been judged solely by the criterion of its general acceptance by Sufis themselves. For this reason no historical, literary or other conventional test can be applied in deciding as to what may be included and what left out.

In accordance with the local culture, the audience and the requirements of the Teaching, Sufis have traditionally made use of appropriate selections from their unparalleled riches of transmitted lore.

In Sufi circles, it is customary for students to soak themselves in stories set for their study, so that the internal dimensions may be unlocked by the teaching master as and when the candidate is judged ready for the experiences which they bring.

At the same time, many Sufi tales have passed into folklore, or ethical teachings, or crept into biographies. Many of them provide nutrition on many levels, and their value as entertainment-pieces alone cannot be denied.

The Three Fishes

THREE fishes once lived in a pool. They were: a clever fish, a half-clever fish and a stupid fish. Life continued for them very much as it is for fishes everywhere until one day came—a man.

He was carrying a net, and the clever fish saw him through the water. Calling upon his experience, the stories he had heard, and his cleverness, he decided to take action.

'There are few places to hide in this pool,' he thought. 'I shall therefore play dead.'

He summoned his strength and jumped out of the pool, landing at the feet of the fisherman, who was rather surprised. But as the clever fish was holding his breath, the fisherman supposed that he was dead: and threw him back. This fish now glided into a small hole under the bank.

Now the second fish, the half-clever one, did not quite understand what had happened. So he swam up to the clever fish and asked him all about it. 'Simple,' said the clever fish, 'I played dead, so he threw me back.'

So the half-clever fish immediately leaped out of the water, at the fisherman's feet. 'Strange,' thought the fisherman, 'they are leaping about all over the place.' And, because the half-clever fish had forgotten to hold his breath the fisherman realized that he was alive and put him into his satchel.

He turned back to peer into the water, and because he had been slightly confused by the fishes jumping on to dry land in front of him, he did not close the flap of his bag. The half-clever fish, when he realized this, was just able to ease himself out and, flipping over and over, got back into the water. He sought out the first fish and lay panting beside him.

Now the third fish, the stupid one, was not able to make anything at all of this, even when he heard the first and second fishes' versions. So they went over every point with him, stressing the importance of not breathing, in order to play dead.

'Thank you so much: *now* I understand,' said the stupid fish. With these words he hurled himself out of the water, landing just beside the fisherman.

Now the fisherman, having lost two fish already, put this one into his bag without bothering to look at whether it was breathing or not. He cast the net again and again into the pool, but the first two fish were crouched into the depression under the bank. And the flap on the fisherman's bag this time was fully closed.

Finally the fisherman gave up. He opened the bag, realized that the stupid fish was not breathing, and took him home for the cat.

໖໖

It is related that Hussein, grandson of Mohammed, transmitted this teaching-story to the Khajagan ('Masters') who in the fourteenth century changed their name to the Naqshbandi Order.

Sometimes the action takes place in a 'world' known as Karatas, the Country of the Black Stone.

This version is from Abdal ('The Transformed One') Afifi. He heard it from Sheikh Mohammed Asghar, who died in 1813. His shrine is in Delhi.

The Food of Paradise

Yunus, the son of Adam, decided one day not only to cast his life in the balance of fate, but to seek the means and reason of the provision of goods for man.

'I am', he said to himself, 'a man. As such I get a portion of the world's goods, every day. This portion comes to me by my own efforts, coupled with the efforts of others. By simplifying this process, I shall find the means whereby sustenance comes to mankind, and learn something about how and why. I shall therefore adopt the religious way, which exhorts man to rely upon almighty God for his sustenance. Rather than live in the world of confusion, where food and other things come apparently through society, I shall throw myself upon the direct support of the Power which rules over all. The beggar depends upon intermediaries: charitable men and women, who are subject to secondary impulses. They give goods or money because they have been trained to do so. I shall accept no such indirect contributions.'

So saying, he walked into the countryside, throwing himself upon the support of invisible forces with the same resolution with which he had accepted the support of visible ones, when he had been a teacher in a school.

He fell asleep, certain that Allah would take complete care of his interests, just as the birds and beasts were catered for in their own realm.

At dawn the bird chorus awakened him, and the son of Adam lay still at first, waiting for his sustenance to appear. In spite of his reliance upon the invisible force and his confidence that he would be able to understand it when it started its operations in the field into which he had thrown himself, he soon realized that speculative thinking alone would not greatly help him in this unusual field.

He was lying at the riverside, and spent the whole day observing nature, peering at the fish in the waters, saying his prayers. From time to time rich and powerful men passed by, accompanied by glitteringly accoutred outriders on the finest horses, harness-bells jingling imperiously to signal their absolute right of way, who merely shouted a salutation at the sight of his venerable turban. Parties of pilgrims paused and chewed dry bread and dried cheese, serving only to sharpen his appetite for the humblest food.

'It is but a test, and all will soon be well,' thought Yunus, as he said his fifth prayer of the day and wrapped himself in contemplation after the manner taught him by a dervish of great perceptive attainments.

Another night passed.

As Yunus sat staring at the sun's broken lights reflected in the mighty Tigris, five hours after dawn on the second day, something bobbing in the reeds caught his eye. This was a packet, enclosed in leaves and bound around with palm-fibre. Yunus, the son of Adam, waded into the river and possessed himself of the unfamiliar cargo.

It weighed about three-quarters of a pound. As he unwound the fibre a delicious smell assailed his nostrils. He was the owner of a quantity of the *halwa* of Baghdad. This halwa, composed of almond paste, rosewater, honey and nuts and other precious elements, was both prized for its taste and esteemed as a health-giving food. Harem beauties nibbled it because of its flavour; warriors carried it on campaigns because of its sustaining power. It was used to treat a hundred ailments.

'My belief is vindicated!' exclaimed Yunus. 'And now for the test. If a similar quantity of halwa, or the equivalent, comes to me upon the waters daily or at other intervals, I shall know the means ordained by providence for my sustenance, and will then only have to use my intelligence to seek the source.'

For the next three days, at exactly the same hour, a packet of halwa floated into Yunus' hands.

This, he decided, was a discovery of the first magnitude. Simplify your circumstances and Nature continued to operate in a roughly similar way. This alone was a discovery which he almost felt impelled to share with the world. For has it not been said: 'When you know, you must teach'? But then he realized that he did not know: he only experienced. The obvious next step was to follow the halwa's course upstream until he arrived at the source. He would then understand not only its origin, but the means whereby it was set aside for his explicit use.

For many days Yunus followed the course of the stream. Each day with the same regularity but at a time correspondingly earlier, the halwa appeared, and he ate it.

Eventually Yunus saw that the river, instead of narrowing as one might expect at the upper part, had widened considerably. In the middle of a broad expanse of water there was a fertile island. On this island stood a mighty and yet beautiful castle. It was from here, he determined, that the food of paradise originated.

As he was considering his next step, Yunus saw that a tall and unkempt dervish, with the matted hair of a hermit and a cloak of multicoloured patches, stood before him.

'Peace, Baba, Father,' he said.

'Ishq, Hoo!' shouted the hermit. 'And what is your business here?'

'I am following a sacred quest,' explained the son of Adam, 'and must in my search reach yonder castle. Have you perhaps an idea how this might be accomplished?'

'As you seem to know nothing about the castle, in spite of having a special interest in it,' answered the hermit, 'I will tell you about it.

'Firstly, the daughter of a king lives there, imprisoned and in exile, attended by numerous beautiful servitors, it is true, but constrained nevertheless. She is unable to escape because the man who captured her and placed her there, because she would not marry him, has erected formidable and inexplicable barriers, invisible to the ordinary eye. You would have to overcome them to enter the castle and find your goal.'

'How can you help me?'

'I am on the point of starting on a special journey of dedication. Here, however, is a word and exercise, the *Wazifa*, which will, if you are worthy, help to summon the invisible powers of the benevolent

Jinns, the creatures of fire, who alone can combat the magical forces which hold the castle locked. Upon you peace.' And he wandered away, after repeating strange sounds and moving with a dexterity and agility truly wonderful in a man of his venerable appearance.

Yunus sat for days practising his Wazifa and watching for the appearance of the halwa. Then, one evening as he looked at the setting sun shining upon a turret of the castle, he saw a strange sight. There, shimmering with unearthly beauty, stood a maiden, who must of course be the princess. She stood for an instant looking into the sun, and then dropped into the waves which lapped far beneath her on to the castle rocks—a packet of halwa. Here, then, was the immediate source of his bounty.

'The source of the Food of Paradise!' cried Yunus. Now he was almost on the very threshold of truth. Sooner or later the Commander of the Jinns, whom through his dervish Wazifa he was calling, must come, and would enable him to reach the castle, the princess, and the truth.

No sooner had these thoughts passed through his mind than he found himself carried away through the skies to what seemed to be an ethereal realm, filled with houses of breathtaking beauty. He entered one, and there stood a creature like a man, who was not a man: young in appearance, yet wise and in some way ageless. 'I', said this vision, 'am the Commander of the Jinns, and I have had thee carried here in answer to thy pleading and the use of those Great Names which were supplied to thee by the Great Dervish. What can I do for thee?'

'O mighty Commander of all the Jinns,' trembled Yunus, 'I am a Seeker of the Truth, and the answer to it is only to be found by me in the enchanted castle near which I was standing when you called me here. Give me, I pray, the power to enter this castle and talk to the imprisoned princess.'

'So shall it be!' exclaimed the Commander. 'But be warned, first of all, that a man gets an answer to his questions in accordance with his fitness to understand and his own preparation.'

'Truth is truth,' said Yunus, 'and I will have it, no matter what it may be. Grant me this boon.'

Soon he was speeding back in a decorporealized form (by the magic of the Jinn) accompanied by a small band of Jinni servitors, charged by their Commander to use their special skills to aid this human being in his quest. In his hand Yunus grasped a special mirror-stone which the Jinn chief had instructed him to turn towards the castle to be able to see the hidden defences.

Through this stone the son of Adam soon found that the castle was protected from assault by a row of giants, invisible but terrible, who smote anyone who approached. Those of the Jinns who were proficient at this task cleared them away. Next he found that there was something like an invisible web or net which hung all around the castle. This, too, was destroyed by the Jinns who flew and who had the special cunning needed to break the net. Finally there was an invisible mass as of stone, which, without making an impression, filled the space between the castle and the river bank. This was overthrown by the skills of the Jinns, who made their salutations and flew fast as light, to their abode.

Yunus looked and saw that a bridge, by its own power, had emerged from the river-bed, and he was able to walk dry shod into the very castle. A soldier at the gate took him immediately to the princess, who was more beautiful even than she had appeared at first.

'We are grateful to you for your services in destroying the defences which made this prison secure,' said the lady. 'And I may now return to my father and want only to reward thee for thy sufferings. Speak, name it, and it shall be given to thee.'

'Incomparable pearl,' said Yunus, 'there is only one thing which I seek, and that is truth. As it is the duty of all who have truth to give it to those who can benefit from it, I adjure you, Highness, to give me the truth which is my need.'

'Speak, and such truth as it is possible to give will freely be thine.'

'Very well, your Highness. How, and by what order, is the Food of Paradise, the wonderful halwa which you throw down every day for me, ordained to be deposited thus?'

'Yunus, son of Adam,' exclaimed the princess, 'the halwa, as you call it, I throw down each day because it is in fact the residue of the cosmetic materials with which I rub myself every day after my bath of asses' milk.'

'I have at last learned', said Yunus, 'that the understanding of a man is conditional upon his capacity to understand. For you, the remains of your daily toilet. For me, the Food of Paradise.'

爻

Only a very few Sufi tales, according to Halqavi (who is the author of 'The Food of Paradise') can be read by anyone at any time and still affect the 'Inner consciousness' constructively.

'Almost all others', he says, 'depend upon where, when and how they are studied. Thus most people will find in them only what they expect to find: entertainment, puzzlement, allegory.'

Yunus, son of Adam, was a Syrian, and died in 1670. He had remarkable healing powers and was an inventor.

When the Waters Were Changed

≈≈≈≈≈≈≈≈≈≈≈≈≈≈≈≈≈≈≈≈≈≈≈≈≈≈≈≈≈≈≈≈≈≈≈≈≈≈

ONCE upon a time Khidr, the Teacher of Moses, called upon mankind with a warning. At a certain date, he said, all the water in the world which had not been specially hoarded, would disappear. It would then be renewed, with different water, which would drive men mad.

Only one man listened to the meaning of this advice. He collected water and went to a secure place where he stored it, and waited for the water to change its character.

On the appointed date the streams stopped running, the wells went dry, and the man who had listened, seeing this happening, went to his retreat and drank his preserved water.

When he saw, from his security, the waterfalls again beginning to flow, this man descended among the other sons of men. He found that they were thinking and talking in an entirely different way from before; yet they had no memory of what had happened, nor of having been warned. When he tried to talk to them, he realized that they thought that he was mad, and they showed hostility or compassion, not understanding.

At first he drank none of the new water, but went back to his concealment, to draw on his supplies, every day. Finally, however, he took the decision to drink the new water because he could not bear the loneliness of living, behaving and thinking in a different way from everyone else. He drank the new water, and became like the rest. Then he forgot all about his own store of special water, and his fellows began to look upon him as a madman who had miraculously been restored to sanity.

≈

TALES OF THE DERVISHES

∞

When the Waters Were Changed

Legend repeatedly links Dhun-Nun, the Egyptian (died 860), reputed author of this tale, with at least one form of Free-masonry. He is, in any case, the earliest figure in the history of the Malamati Dervish Order, which has often been stated by Western students to have striking similarities with the craft of the Masons. Dhun-Nun, it is said, rediscovered the meaning of the Pharaonic hieroglyphics.

This version is attributed to Sayed Sabir Ali-Shah, a saint of the Chishti Order, who died in 1818.

The Tale of the Sands

A STREAM, from its source in far-off mountains, passing through every kind and description of countryside, at last reached the sands of the desert. Just as it had crossed every other barrier, the stream tried to cross this one, but it found that as fast as it ran into the sand, its waters disappeared.

It was convinced, however, that its destiny was to cross this desert, and yet there was no way. Now a hidden voice, coming from the desert itself, whispered: 'The Wind crosses the desert, and so can the stream.'

The stream objected that it was dashing itself against the sand, and only getting absorbed: that the wind could fly, and this was why it could cross a desert.

'By hurtling in your own accustomed way you cannot get across. You will either disappear or become a marsh. You must allow the wind to carry you over, to your destination.'

But how could this happen? 'By allowing yourself to be absorbed in the wind.'

This idea was not acceptable to the stream. After all, it had never been absorbed before. It did not want to lose its individuality. And, once having lost it, how was one to know that it could ever be regained?

'The wind', said the sand, 'performs this function. It takes up water, carries it over the desert, and then lets it fall again. Falling as rain, the water again becomes a river.'

'How can I know that this is true?'

'It is so, and if you do not believe it, you cannot become more than a quagmire, and even that could take many, many years; and it certainly is not the same as a stream.'

'But can I not remain the same stream that I am today?'

'You cannot in either case remain so,' the whisper said. 'Your essential part is carried away and forms a stream again. You are called what you are even today because you do not know which part of you is the essential one.'

When he heard this, certain echoes began to arise in the thoughts of the stream. Dimly, he remembered a state in which he—or some part of him, was it?—had been held in the arms of a wind. He also remembered—or did he?—that this was the real thing, not necessarily the obvious thing, to do.

And the stream raised his vapour into the welcoming arms of the wind, which gently and easily bore it upwards and along, letting it fall softly as soon as they reached the roof of a mountain, many, many miles away. And because he had had his doubts, the stream was able to remember and record more strongly in his mind the details of the experience. He reflected, 'Yes, now I have learned my true identity.'

The stream was learning. But the sands whispered: 'We know, because we see it happen day after day: and because we, the sands, extend from the riverside all the way to the mountain.'

And that is why it is said that the way in which the Stream of Life is to continue on its journey is written in the Sands.

ॐ

This beautiful story is current in verbal tradition in many languages, almost always circulating among dervishes and their pupils.

It was used in Sir Fairfax Cartwright's *Mystic Rose from the Garden of the King*, published in Britain in 1899.

The present version is from Awad Afifi the Tunisian, who died in 1870.

The Blind Ones and the Matter of the Elephant

BEYOND Ghor there was a city. All its inhabitants were blind. A king with his entourage arrived near by; he brought his army and camped in the desert. He had a mighty elephant, which he used in attack and to increase the people's awe.

The populace became anxious to see the elephant, and some sightless from among this blind community ran like fools to find it.

As they did not even know the form or shape of the elephant they groped sightlessly, gathering information by touching some part of it.

Each thought that he knew something, because he could feel a part.

When they returned to their fellow-citizens eager groups clustered around them. Each of these was anxious, misguidedly, to learn the truth from those who were themselves astray.

They asked about the form, the shape of the elephant: and listened to all that they were told.

The man whose hand had reached an ear was asked about the elephant's nature. He said: 'It is a large, rough thing, wide and broad, like a rug.'

And the one who had felt the trunk said: 'I have the real facts about it. It is like a straight and hollow pipe, awful and destructive.'

The one who had felt its feet and legs said: 'It is mighty and firm, like a pillar.'

Each had felt one part out of many. Each had perceived it wrongly. No mind knew all: knowledge is not the companion of the blind. All imagined something, something incorrect.

The created is not informed about divinity. There is no Way in this science by means of the ordinary intellect.

ᴂ

The Blind Ones and the Matter of the Elephant

This tale is more famous in Rumi's version — 'The Elephant in the Dark House', found in the *Mathnavi*. Rumi's teacher Hakim Sanai gives this earlier treatment in the first book of his Sufi classic *The Walled Garden of Truth*. He died in 1150.

Both stories are themselves renderings of a similar argument which, according to tradition, has been used by Sufi teaching masters for many centuries.

The Dog, the Stick and the Sufi

A MAN dressed as a Sufi was walking along one day when he saw a dog on the road, which he struck hard with his staff. The dog, yelping with pain, ran to the great sage Abu-Said. Throwing himself at his feet and holding up his injured paw, he called for justice against the Sufi who had maltreated him so cruelly.

The wise one called them together. To the Sufi he said: 'O heedless one! How is it possible for you to treat a dumb animal in this manner. Look at what you have done!'

The Sufi answered: 'Far from its being my fault, it is that of the dog. I did not strike him from a mere whim, but for the reason that he had fouled my robe.'

But the dog persisted in his complaint.

Then the peerless one addressed the dog: 'Rather than waiting for the Ultimate Compensation, allow me to give you a compensation for your pain.'

The dog said: 'Great and wise one! When I saw this man garbed as a Sufi, I was able to conclude that he would do me no harm. Had I seen instead a man wearing ordinary dress, I would naturally have given him a wide berth. My real mistake was to assume that the outward appearance of a man of truth indicated safety. If you desire his punishment, take away from him the garment of the Elect. Deprive him of the costume of the People of Righteousness ... '

The dog himself was of a certain Rank in the Way. It is wrong to believe that a man *must* be better than he.

ɷ

လလ

The Dog, the Stick and the Sufi

The 'conditioning' which is represented here by the Robe of the Dervish is often mistaken by esotericists and religious people of all kinds as something connected with real experience or worth.

This tale, from Attar's *Divine Book* (the *Ilahi-Nama*), is often repeated by the dervishes of the 'Path of Blame', and ascribed to Hamdun the Bleacher, in the ninth century.

How to Catch Monkeys

ONCE upon a time there was a monkey who was very fond of cherries. One day he saw a delicious-looking cherry, and came down from his tree to get it. But the fruit turned out to be in a clear glass bottle. After some experimentation, the monkey found that he could get hold of the cherry by putting his hand into the bottle by way of the neck. As soon as he had done so, he closed his hand over the cherry; but then he found that he could not withdraw his fist holding the cherry, because it was larger than the internal dimension of the neck.

Now all this was deliberate, because the cherry in the bottle was a trap laid by a monkey-hunter who knew how monkeys think.

The hunter, hearing the monkey's whimperings, came along and the monkey tried to run away. But, because his hand was, as he thought, stuck in the bottle, he could not move fast enough to escape.

But, as he thought, he still had hold of the cherry. The hunter picked him up. A moment later he tapped the monkey sharply on the elbow, making him suddenly relax his hold on the fruit.

The monkey was free, but he was captured. The hunter had used the cherry and the bottle, but he still had them.

৵৵

This is one of the many tales of the tradition collectively called the *Book of Amu Daria*.

The Amu or Jihun River of Central Asia is known to modern cartographers as the Oxus. Somewhat confusingly for the literal-minded, it is a dervish term for certain materials like this story, and also for an anonymous group of itinerant teachers whose headquarters is near Aubshaur, in the Hindu-Kush mountains of Afghanistan.

This version is told by Khwaja Ali Ramitani, who died in 1306.

The Ancient Coffer of Nuri Bey

Nuri Bey was a reflective and respected Albanian, who had married a wife much younger than himself.

One evening when he had returned home earlier than usual, a faithful servant came to him and said:

'Your wife, our mistress, is acting suspiciously.

'She is in her apartments with a huge chest, large enough to hold a man, which belonged to your grandmother.

'It should contain only a few ancient embroideries.

'I believe that there may now be much more in it.

'She will not allow me, your oldest retainer, to look inside.'

Nuri went to his wife's room, and found her sitting disconsolately beside the massive wooden box.

'Will you show me what is in the chest?' he asked.

'Because of the suspicion of a servant, or because you do not trust me?'

'Would it not be easier just to open it, without thinking about the undertones?' asked Nuri.

'I do not think it possible.'

'Is it locked?'

'Yes.'

'Where is the key?'

She held it up, 'Dismiss the servant and I will give it to you.'

The servant was dismissed. The woman handed over the key and herself withdrew, obviously troubled in mind.

Nuri Bey thought for a long time. Then he called four gardeners from his estate. Together they carried the chest by night unopened to a distant part of the grounds, and buried it.

The matter was never referred to again.

ౚ

The Ancient Coffer of Nuri Bey

This tantalizing story, repeatedly stressed as being of interior significance aside from its evident moral, is part of the repertoire of wandering (Kalandar) dervishes, whose patron saint is the thirteenth-century Yusuf of Andalusia.

They were formerly numerous in Turkey. This tale has found its way, in an expanded form, into English through H. G. Dwight's *Stambul Nights*, published in the United States in 1916 and 1922.

The Three Truths

THE Sufis are known as Seekers of the Truth, this truth being a knowledge of objective reality. An ignorant and covetous tyrant once determined to possess himself of this truth. He was called Rudarigh*, a great lord of Murcia in Spain. He decided that truth was something which Omar el-Alawi of Tarragona could be forced to tell him.

Omar was arrested and brought to the Court. Rudarigh said: 'I have ordained that the truths which you know are to be told to me in words which I understand, otherwise your life is forfeit.'

Omar answered: 'Do you observe in this chivalric Court the universal custom whereby if an arrested person tells the truth in answer to a question and that truth does not inculpate him, he is released to freedom?'

'That is so,' said the lord.

'I call upon all of you here present to witness this, by the honour of our lord,' said Omar, 'and I will now tell you not one truth, but three.'

'We must also be satisfied,' said Rudarigh, 'that what you claim to be these truths are in fact truth. The proof must accompany the telling.'

'For such a lord as you,' said Omar, 'to whom we can give not one truth but three, we can also give truths which will be self-evident.'

Rudarigh preened himself at this compliment.

'The first truth', said the Sufi, 'is — "I am he who is called Omar the Sufi of Tarragona." The second is that you have agreed to release me if I tell the truth. The third is that you wish to know the truth as you conceive it.'

* Roderick. Roderigo.

33

Such was the impression caused by these words that the tyrant was compelled to give the dervish his freedom.

⋙⋘

This story introduces dervish oral legends traditionally composed by el-Mutanabbi. These, he stipulated, according to the tellers, should not be written down for 1,000 years.

El-Mutanabbi, one of the greatest Arabic poets, died a thousand years ago.

One of the features of this collection is that it is considered to be under constant revision, because of its perpetual retelling in accordance with 'the changes of the times'.

The Sultan Who Became an Exile

A SULTAN of Egypt, it is related, called a conference of learned men, and very soon — as is usually the case — a dispute arose. The subject was the Night Journey of the Prophet Mohammed. It is said that on that occasion the Prophet was taken from his bed up into the celestial spheres. During this period he saw paradise and hell, conferred with God ninety thousand times, had many other experiences — and was returned to his room while his bed was yet warm. A pot of water which had been overturned by the flight and spilled was still not empty when the Prophet returned.

Some held that this was possible, by a different measurement of time. The Sultan claimed that it was impossible.

The sages said that all things were possible to divine power. This did not satisfy the king.

The news of this conflict came at length to the Sufi sheikh Shahabudin, who immediately presented himself at Court. The Sultan showed due humility to the teacher, who said: 'I intend to proceed without further delay to my demonstration: for know now that both the interpretations of the problem are incorrect, and that there are demonstrable factors which can account for traditions without the need to resort to crude speculation or insipid and uninformed "logicality".'

There were four windows in the audience-chamber. The sheikh ordered one to be opened. The Sultan looked out of it. On a mountain beyond he saw an invading army, a myriad, bearing down on the palace. He was terribly afraid.

'Pray forget it: for it is nothing,' said the sheikh.

He shut the window and opened it again. This time there was not a soul to be seen.

When he opened another of the windows, the city outside was seen to be consumed by flames. The Sultan cried out in alarm.

'Do not distress yourself, Sultan, for it is nothing,' said the sheikh. When he had closed and again opened the window, there was no fire to be seen.

The third window being opened revealed a flood approaching the palace. Then, again, there was no flood.

When the fourth window was opened, instead of the customary desert, a garden of paradise was revealed—and then, by the shutting of the window, the scene vanished as before.

Now the sheikh ordered a vessel of water to be brought, and the Sultan to put his head into it for a moment. As soon as he had done so, the Sultan found himself alone on a deserted seashore, a place which he did not know.

At this magic spell of the treacherous sheikh he was transported with fury, and vowed vengeance.

Soon he met some woodcutters who asked him who he was. Unable to explain his true state, he told them that he was shipwrecked. They gave him some clothes, and he walked to a town where a blacksmith, seeing him aimlessly wandering, asked him who he was. 'A shipwrecked merchant, dependent upon the charity of woodcutters, now with no resources,' answered the Sultan.

The man then told him about a custom of that country. All newcomers could ask the first woman who left the bath-house to marry him, and she would be obliged to do so. He went to the bath, and saw a beautiful maiden leaving. He asked her if she was married already: and she was, so he had to ask the next, an ugly one. And the next. The fourth was really exquisite. She said that she was not married, but pushed past him, affronted by his miserable appearance and dress.

Suddenly a man stood before him and said: 'I have been sent to find a bedraggled man here. Please follow me.'

The Sultan followed the servant, and was shown into a wonderful house in one of whose sumptuous apartments he sat for hours. Finally four beautiful and gorgeously attired women came in, preceding a fifth, even more beautiful. She the Sultan recognized as the last woman whom he had approached at the bath-house.

She welcomed him and explained that she had hurried home to prepare for his coming, and that her hauteur was only one of the customs of the country, practised by all women in the street.

Then followed a magnificent meal. Wonderful robes were brought and given to the Sultan, while delicate music was played.

The Sultan stayed seven years with his new wife: until they had squandered all her patrimony. Then the woman told him that he must now provide for her and their seven sons.

Recalling his first friend in the city, the Sultan returned to the blacksmith for counsel. Since the Sultan had no trade or training, he was advised to go to the marketplace and offer his services as a porter.

In one day he earned, through carrying a terrible load, only one-tenth of the money which was needed for the food of the family.

The following day the Sultan made his way to the seashore again, where he found the very spot from which he had emerged seven long years before. Deciding to say his prayers, he started to wash in the water: when he suddenly and dramatically found himself back at the palace, with the vessel of water, the sheikh and his courtiers.

'Seven years of exile, evil man!' roared the Sultan. 'Seven years, a family and having to be a porter! Have you no fear of God, the Almighty, for this deed?'

'But it is only a moment', said the Sufi master, 'since you put your head into this water.'

His courtiers bore out this statement.

The Sultan could not possibly bring himself to believe a word of this. He started to give the order for the beheading of the sheikh. Perceiving by inner sense that this was to happen, the sheikh exercised the capacity called *Ilm el-Ghaibat*: The Science of Absence. This caused him to be instantly and corporeally transported to Damascus, many days' distance away.

From here he wrote a letter to the king:

'Seven years passed for you, as you will now have discovered, during an instant of your head in the water. This happens through the exercise of certain faculties, and carries no special significance

37

except that it is illustrative of what can happen. Was not the bed warm, was not the water-jar empty in the tradition?

'It is not whether a thing has happened or not which is the important element. It is possible for anything to happen. What is, however, important, is the significance of the happening. In your case, there was no significance. In the case of the Prophet, there was significance in the happening.'

တ

It is stated that every passage in the Koran has seven meanings, each applicable to the state of the reader or listener.

This tale, like many others of the Sufi kind, emphasizes the dictum of Mohammed: 'Speak to everyone in accordance with the degree of his understanding.'

The Sufi method, according to Ibrahim Khawwas, is: 'Demonstrate the unknown in terms of what is called "known" by the audience.'

This version is from the manuscript called *Hu-Nama* (Book of Hu), in the collection of the Nawab of Sardhana, dated 1596.

The Story of Fire

ᔕᔕᔕᔕᔕᔕᔕᔕᔕᔕᔕᔕᔕᔕᔕᔕᔕᔕᔕᔕᔕᔕᔕᔕᔕᔕᔕᔕᔕᔕ

ONCE upon a time a man was contemplating the ways in which Nature operates, and he discovered, because of his concentration and application, how fire could be made.

This man was called Nour. He decided to travel from one community to another, showing people his discovery.

Nour passed the secret to many groups of people. Some took advantage of the knowledge. Others drove him away, thinking that he must be dangerous, before they had had time to understand how valuable this discovery could be to them. Finally, a tribe before which he demonstrated became so panic-stricken that they set about him and killed him, being convinced that he was a demon.

Centuries passed. The first tribe which had learned about fire reserved the secret for their priests, who remained in affluence and power while the people froze.

The second tribe forgot the art and worshipped instead the instruments. The third worshipped a likeness of Nour himself, because it was he who had taught them. The fourth retained the story of the making of fire in their legends: some believed them, some did not. The fifth community really did use fire, and this enabled them to be warmed, to cook their food, and to manufacture all kinds of useful articles.

After many, many years, a wise man and a small band of his disciples were travelling through the lands of these tribes. The disciples were amazed at the variety of rituals which they encountered; and one and all said to their teacher: 'But all these procedures are in fact related to the making of fire, nothing else. We should reform these people!'

The teacher said: 'Very well, then. We shall restart our journey.

By the end of it, those who survive will know the real problems and how to approach them.'

When they reached the first tribe, the band was hospitably received. The priests invited the travellers to attend their religious ceremony, the making of fire. When it was over, and the tribe was in a state of excitement at the event which they had witnessed, the master said: 'Does anyone wish to speak?'

The first disciple said: 'In the cause of Truth I feel myself constrained to say something to these people.'

'If you will do so at your own risk, you may do so,' said the master.

Now the disciple stepped forward in the presence of the tribal chief and his priests and said: 'I can perform the miracle which you take to be a special manifestation of deity. If I do so, will you accept that you have been in error for so many years?'

But the priests cried: 'Seize him!' and the man was taken away, never to be seen again.

The travellers went to the next territory where the second tribe were worshipping the instruments of fire-making. Again a disciple volunteered to try to bring reason to the community.

With the permission of the master, he said: 'I beg permission to speak to you as reasonable people. You are worshipping the means whereby something may be done, not even the thing itself. Thus you are suspending the advent of its usefulness. I know the reality that lies at the basis of this ceremony.'

This tribe was composed of more reasonable people. But they said to the disciple: 'You are welcome as a traveller and stranger in our midst. But, as a stranger, foreign to our history and customs, you cannot understand what we are doing. You make a mistake Perhaps, even, you are trying to take away or alter our religion. We therefore decline to listen to you.'

The travellers moved on.

When they arrived in the land of the third tribe, they found before every dwelling an idol representing Nour, the original firemaker. The third disciple addressed the chiefs of the tribe:

'This idol represents a man, who represents a capacity, which can be used.'

'This may be so,' answered the Nour-worshippers, 'but the penetration of the real secret is only for the few.'

'It is only for the few who will understand, not for those who refuse to face certain facts,' said the third disciple.

'This is rank heresy, and from a man who does not even speak our language correctly, and is not a priest ordained in our faith,' muttered the priests. And he could make no headway.

The band continued their journey, and arrived in the land of the fourth tribe. Now a fourth disciple stepped forward in the assembly of the people.

'The story of making fire is true, and I know how it may be done,' he said.

Confusion broke out within the tribe, which split into various factions. Some said: 'This may be true, and if it is, we want to find out how to make fire.' When these people were examined by the master and his followers, however, it was found that most of them were anxious to use firemaking for personal advantage, and did not realize that it was something for human progress. So deep had the distorted legends penetrated into the minds of most people that those who thought that they might in fact represent truth were often unbalanced ones, who could not have made fire even if they had been shown how.

There was another faction, who said: 'Of course the legends are not true. This man is just trying to fool us, to make a place for himself here.'

And a further faction said: 'We prefer the legends as they are, for they are the very mortar of our cohesion. If we abandon them, and we find that this new interpretation is useless, what will become of our community then?'

And there were other points of view, as well.

So the party travelled on, until they reached the lands of the fifth community, where firemaking was a commonplace, and where other preoccupations faced them.

The master said to his disciples:

'You have to learn how to teach, for man does not want to be taught. First of all, you will have to teach people how to learn. And before that you have to teach them that there is still something to be learned. They imagine that they are ready to learn. But they want to learn what they *imagine* is to be learned, not what they have first to learn. When you have learned all this, then you can devise the way to teach. Knowledge without special capacity to teach is not the same as knowledge and capacity.'

ᏡᏡ

Ahmed el-Bedavi (died 1276) is reputed to have said, in answer to the question: 'What is a barbarian?':

'A barbarian is one whose perceptions are so insensitive that he thinks that he can understand by thinking or feeling something which can be perceived only through development and constant application to the striving towards God.

'Men laugh at Moses and Jesus, either because they are utterly insensitive, or because they have concealed from themselves what these people really meant when they talked and acted.'

According to dervish lore, he was accused of preaching Christianity by Moslems, but repudiated by Christians because he refused to accept later Christian dogma literally. He was the founder of the Egyptian Bedavi Order.

The Ogre and the Sufi

A SUFI master travelling alone through a desolate mountain region was suddenly faced by an ogre—a giant ghoul, who told him that he was going to destroy him. The master said, 'Very well, try if you like, but I can overcome you, for I am immensely powerful in more ways than you think.' 'Nonsense,' said the ghoul. 'You are a Sufi master, interested in spiritual things. You cannot overcome me, because I rely upon brute force, and I am thirty times larger than you.'

'If you want a trial of strength,' said the Sufi, 'take this stone and squeeze liquid out of it.' He picked up a small piece of rock and handed it to the apparition. Try as he might, the ghoul could not. 'It is impossible; there is no water in this stone. You show me if there is.' In the half-darkness, the master took the stone, took an egg out of his pocket, and squeezed the two together, holding his hand over that of the ghoul. The ghoul was impressed; for people are often impressed by things that they do not understand, and value such things highly, more highly than they should in their own interests.

'I must think this over,' he said. 'Come to my cave, and I shall give you hospitality for the night.' The Sufi accompanied him to an immense cave, strewn with the belongings of thousands of murdered travellers, a veritable Aladdin's cavern. 'Lie here beside me and sleep,' said the ghoul, 'and we will try conclusions in the morning.' He lay down and immediately fell asleep.

The master, instinctively warned of treachery, suddenly felt a prompting to get up and conceal himself at some distance from the ghoul. This he did, after arranging the bed to give the impression that he was still in it.

No sooner was he sat a safe distance than the ghoul awoke. He picked up a tree-trunk with one hand, and dealt the dummy in the bed seven mighty clouts. Then he lay down again and went to sleep. The master returned to his bed, lay down, and called to the ghoul:

'O ghoul! This cavern of yours is comfortable, but I have been bitten seven times by a mosquito. You really should do something about it.'

This shocked the ghoul so much that he dared not attempt a further attack. After all, if a man had been hit seven times by a ghoul wielding a tree trunk with all the force he had ...

In the morning the ghoul threw the Sufi a whole ox-skin and said: 'Bring some water for breakfast, so that we can make tea.' Instead of picking up the skin (which he could hardly have lifted in any case) the master walked to the near-by stream and started to dig a small channel towards the cave. The ghoul was getting thirsty: 'Why don't you bring the water?' 'Patience, my friend. I am making a permanent channel to bring the spring-water right to the mouth of the cavern, so that you will never have to carry a water-skin.' But the ghoul was too thirsty to wait. Picking up the skin, he strode to the river and filled it himself. When the tea was made he drank several gallons, and his reasoning faculties began to work a little better. 'If you are so strong—and you have given me proof of it—why can't you dig that channel faster, instead of inch by inch?'

'Because', said the master, 'nothing which is truly worth doing can be properly done without the expenditure of a minimum amount of effort. Everything has its own quantity of effort; and I am applying the minimum necessary effort to the digging of the canal. Besides, I knew that you are such a creature of habit that you will always use the ox-skin.'

৩৫১

This story is often heard in teahouses in Central Asia, and resembles folkloric tales of the Europe of the Middle Ages.

The present version is from a *Majmua* (dervish collection) originally written by Hikayati in the eleventh century, according to the colophon, but in the form given here apparently dating from the sixteenth century.

The Merchant and the Christian Dervish

A RICH merchant of Tabriz came to Konia, looking for the wisest man there, for he was in trouble. After trying to get advice from the religious leaders, the lawyers and others, he heard of Rumi, to whom he was taken.

He took with him fifty gold pieces as an offering. When he saw the Maulana in the audition-hall, he was overcome with emotion. Jalaludin said to him:

'Your fifty coins are accepted. But you have lost two hundred, which is why you are here. God has punished you and is showing you something. Now all will be well with you.'

The merchant was amazed at what the Maulana knew. Rumi continued:

'You have had many troubles because one day in the far west of Christendom you saw a Christian dervish lying in the street. You spat at him. Go to him and ask forgiveness, and give him our salutations.'

As the merchant stood terrified at this reading of his mind, Jalaludin said: 'Shall we show him to you now?' He touched the wall of the room, and the merchant saw the scene of the saint in the market place in Europe. He reeled away from the Master's presence, completely nonplussed.

Travelling as fast as he could to the Christian sage, he found him lying prostrate on the ground. As he approached him, the Frankish dervish said: 'Our Master Jalal has communicated with me.'

The merchant looked in the direction in which the dervish was pointing, and saw, as in a picture, Jalaludin chanting such words as these: 'Whether a ruby or a pebble, there is a place on His hill, there is a place for all … '

The merchant carried back the greetings of the Frankish saint to Jalal, and settled down in the community of the dervishes at Konia.

茲

The extent of Jalaludin Rumi's influence upon the thought and literature of the West is today slowly becoming apparent through academic research. There is no doubt that he had many western disciples, and his stories appear in the Hans Andersen tales, in the *Gesta Romanorum* of 1324, even in Shakespeare.

In the East there is considerable traditional insistence upon his close connection with western mystics and thinkers. This version of 'The Merchant and the Christian Dervish' is translated from Aflaki's *Munaqib el-Arifin*, the lives of early Mevlevi dervishes, completed in 1353.

The Golden Fortune

ONCE upon a time there was a merchant named Abdul Malik. He was known as the Good Man of Khorasan, because from his immense fortune he used to give to charity and hold feasts for the poor.

But one day it occurred to him that he was simply giving away some of what he had; and that the pleasure which he obtained through his generosity was far in excess of what it really cost him to sacrifice what was after all such a small proportion of his wealth. As soon as this thought entered his mind, he decided to give away every penny for the good of mankind. And he did so.

No sooner had he divested himself of all his possessions, resigned to face whatever events life might have in store for him, Abdul Malik saw, during his meditation-hour, a strange figure seem to rise from the floor of his room. A man was taking shape before his very eyes, dressed in the patchwork robe of the mysterious dervish.

'O Abdul Malik, generous man of Khorasan!' intoned the apparition. 'I am your real self, which has now become almost real to you because you have done something really charitable measured against which your previous record of goodness is as nothing. Because of this, and because you were able to part with your fortune without feeling personal satisfaction, I am rewarding you from the real source of reward.

'In future, I will appear before you in this way every day. You will strike me; and I will turn into gold. You will be able to take from this golden image as much as you may wish. Do not fear that you will harm me, because whatever you take will be replaced from the source of all endowments.'

So saying, he disappeared.

The very next morning a friend named Bay-Akal was sitting with Abdul Malik when the dervish spectre began to manifest itself. Abdul Malik struck it with a stick, and the figure fell to the ground, transformed into gold. He took part of it for himself and gave some of the gold to his guest.

Now Bay-Akal, not knowing what had gone before, started to think how he could perform a similar wonder. He knew that dervishes had strange powers and concluded that it was necessary only to beat them to obtain gold.

So he arranged for a feast to be held to which every dervish who heard of it could come and eat his fill. When they had all eaten well, Bay-Akal took up an iron bar and thrashed every dervish within reach until they lay battered and broken on the ground.

Those dervishes who were unharmed seized Bay-Akal and took him to the judge. They stated their case and produced the wounded dervishes as evidence. Bay-Akal related what had happened at Abdul Malik's house and explained his reasons for trying to reproduce the trick.

Abdul Malik was called, and on the way to the court his golden self whispered to him what to say.

'May it please the court,' he said, 'this man seems to me to be insane, or to be trying to cover up some penchant for assaulting people without cause. I do know him, but his story does not correspond with my own experiences in my house.'

Bay-Akal was therefore placed for a time in a lunatic asylum, until he became more calm. The dervishes recovered almost at once, through some science known to themselves. And nobody believed that such an astonishing thing as a man who becomes a golden statue—and daily at that—could ever take place.

For many another year, until he was gathered to his forefathers, Abdul Malik continued to break the image which was himself, and to distribute its treasure, which was himself, to those whom he could not help in any other way than materially.

ॐ

There is a dervish tradition that clerics present their morally uplifting teachings in parable form, but that dervishes conceal their teachings more completely; because only the effort to understand, or the efforts of a teaching master, will create the effect which will really help transform the hearer.

This tale inclines more towards the parable form than most of its kind. But the dervish who related it in the market-place of Peshawar in the early nineteen fifties warned: 'Do not take the moral: concentrate upon the early part of the story. It tells you about method.'

The Candlestick of Iron

ᖉᖉᖉᖉᖉᖉᖉᖉᖉᖉᖉᖉᖉᖉᖉᖉᖉᖉᖉᖉᖉᖉᖉᖉᖉᖉ

ONCE upon a time a poor widow was looking out of the window of her house when she saw a humble dervish coming along the road. He seemed weary beyond endurance, and his patchwork robe was covered in grime. It was evident that he needed some help.

Running into the street, the woman called out: 'Noble Dervish, I know that you are one of the Elect, but there must be times when even such insignificant persons as myself can be of use to the Seekers. Come and rest in my house; for is it not said: "Whoever helps the Friends will himself be helped, and who hinders them will be hindered, although how and when is a mystery." '

'Thank you, good woman,' said the dervish, and he entered the cottage, where in a few days he was rested and much restored.

Now this woman had a son named Abdullah, who had had few chances of advancement because he had spent most of his life cutting wood to sell at the local market and was not able to extend his experiences of life in such a manner as to enable him to help either himself or his mother.

The dervish said to him: 'My child, I am a man of learning, helpless though I may look. Come, be my companion and I will share great opportunities with you, if your mother agrees.'

The mother was only too glad to allow her son to travel with the sage, and the two set off along the road together.

When they had travelled through many countries and endured much together, the dervish said: 'Abdullah, we have reached the end of a road. I shall perform certain rituals which, should they receive favourable acceptance, will cause the earth to open and reveal something the like of which is given to few men. This is a treasure, concealed here many years ago. Are you afraid?'

Abdullah agreed to try, and swore to remain constant, no matter what might happen.

The dervish now performed certain strange movements, and muttered many sounds, in which Abdullah joined him: and the earth opened.

The dervish said: 'Now, Abdullah, listen carefully, paying complete attention. You have to descend into the vault which is exposed before us. Your task is to possess yourself of a candlestick made of iron. You will see before you arrive at it treasures the like of which have seldom been revealed to man. Ignore them, for it is the iron candlestick alone which is your goal and aim. As soon as you find it, bring it back here.'

Abdullah went down into the treasure vault and sure enough there were so many sparkling jewels, so many plates of gold, such amazing treasures which cannot be described because there are no words for them, that he was completely bemused. Forgetting the words of the dervish he filled his arms with the most glittering prizes he could see.

And then he saw the candlestick. Thinking that he might as well take it to the dervish, and that he could conceal in his wide sleeves enough gold for himself, he took it up, and remounted the steps which led to the surface of the earth. But when he came out of the hole, he found that he was near the cottage of his mother, and the dervish was nowhere to be found.

As soon as he tried to show his gold and ornaments to his mother, they seemed to melt away and disappeared. Only the candlestick was left. Abdullah examined it. There were twelve branches, and he lit a candle in one of them. Suddenly a figure like a dervish seemed to appear. The apparition gyrated a little and then put a small coin on the ground and disappeared again.

Now Abdullah lit all twelve candles. Twelve dervishes materialized, moved in rhythm for an hour and threw him twelve coins before they vanished.

When they had recovered from their amazement, Abdullah and his mother realized that they could live quite well on the yield of the candlestick, for they discovered that they could obtain twelve pieces of silver each day from the 'dance of the dervishes'. But before very long Abdullah thought of the incalculable riches which he had seen in the subterraneous cavern, and decided to see whether he could have another chance of getting some real wealth for himself.

He searched and searched, but could not find the place where the entrance of the cave was. By now, however, he had become obsessed by the desire to become rich. He set off and travelled through the world until he came to a palace which was the home of the miserable dervish whom his mother had once found tottering near her home.

This search had occupied many months, and Abdullah was pleased when he was ushered into the presence of the dervish, whom he found to be dressed like a king and surrounded by a horde of disciples.

'Now,' said the dervish, 'you ungrateful one! I will show you what this candlestick can really do' And he took up a stick and struck the candlestick, whereupon each branch turned into a treasure greater than all that the boy had seen in the cavern. The dervish had the gold, the silver and the jewels taken away to be distributed to worthy people, and lo, the candlestick was seen to be standing there again, ready to be used anew.

'Now,' said the dervish, 'since you cannot be trusted to do things properly, and because you have betrayed your trust, you must leave me. But, because you have at least returned the candlestick, you may have a camel and a load of gold for yourself.'

Abdullah stayed at the palace overnight, and in the morning he was able to hide the candlestick in the saddle of the camel. As soon as he got home he lighted the candles, and he struck the whole thing with a stick.

But he had still not learned how the magic was accomplished; for, instead of using his right hand to hold the stick, he used his left. The twelve dervishes immediately appeared, picked up the gold and jewels, saddled the camel, seized the candlestick and vanished. And Abdullah was worse off than before, for he still had the memory of his ineptitude, his ingratitude, his theft and his nearness to riches.

But he never had another chance again, and he was never again wholly at ease in his mind.

∞

This tale was set in a Sufi school, as a 'development-exercise' for a number of students who were regarded as too literal-minded. It refers in a disguised form to certain dervish exercises, and indicates that harm or uselessness may befall those who carry out mystical procedures without having overcome certain personal propensities.

Strike on this Spot

DHUN-NUN the Egyptian explained graphically in a parable how he extracted knowledge concealed in Pharaonic inscriptions.

There was a statue with pointing finger, upon which was inscribed: 'Strike on this spot for treasure.' Its origin was unknown, but generations of people had hammered the place marked by the sign. Because it was made of the hardest stone, little impression was made on it, and the meaning remained cryptic.

Dhun-Nun, wrapped in contemplation of the statue, one day exactly at midday observed that the *shadow* of the pointing finger, unnoticed for centuries, followed a line in the paving beneath the statue.

Marking the place he obtained the necessary instruments and prised up by chisel-blows the flagstone, which proved to be the trapdoor in the roof of a subterranean cave which contained strange articles of a workmanship which enabled him to deduce the science of their manufacture, long since lost, and hence to acquire the treasures and those of a more formal kind which accompanied them.

∞

Almost the same story is told by Pope Sylvester II, who brought 'Arabian' learning, including mathematics, from Seville in Spain in the tenth century.

Reputedly a magician because of his technical attainments, Gerbert (as he was originally called) 'lodged with a philosopher of the Saracen sect'. It was almost certainly here that he learned this Sufi tale.

It is said to have been passed on by the Caliph Abu-Bakr, who died in 634.

Why the Clay Birds Flew Away

ONE day Jesus, the son of Mary, while a child, was fashioning small birds out of clay. Some other youngsters who could not do so ran to the elders and told them, with many complaints. The elders said: 'This work cannot be allowed on the Sabbath,' for it was a Saturday.

Accordingly they went to the pool where the Son of Mary was sitting and asked him where his birds were. For answer he pointed to the birds which had been fashioned: and they flew away.

'Making birds which fly is impossible, therefore it cannot be a breaking of the Sabbath,' said one elder.

'I would learn this art,' said another.

'This is no art, it is but deception,' said a third.

So the Sabbath was not broken, the art could not be taught. As for deception, the elders as well as the children had deceived themselves, because they did not know what the object of the fashioning of the birds was.

The reason for doing no work on Saturday had been forgotten. The knowledge of what is a deception and what is not was imperfect to those elders. The beginning of art and the end of action was unknown to them: thus it was also with the lengthening of the plank of wood.

It is further related that one day Jesus, the son of Mary, was in the workshop of Joseph the Carpenter. When a plank of wood was found to be too short, Jesus pulled it, and it was found to have become in some way lengthened.

When this story was told to the people, some said: 'This is a miracle, therefore this child will be a saint.'

Others said: 'We do not believe it, do it again for us.'

A third party said: 'This cannot be true, therefore exclude it from the books.'

The three parties, with their different feelings, yet got the same answer because none knew the purpose and the real significance lying within the statement: 'He stretched a plank.'

৹৵৹

Sufi authors make frequent reference to Jesus as a Master of the Way. There is, in addition, an enormous body of oral tradition about him current in the Middle East, which awaits a collector. This tale is found, in slightly different forms, in more than one dervish collection. Sufis say that 'Son of a Carpenter' and other vocational names given to Gospel characters are initiatory terms, not necessarily describing the individual's work.

The Gnat Namouss—and the Elephant

ONCE upon a time there was a gnat. His name was Namouss, and he was known, because of his sensitivity, as Perceptive Namouss. Namouss decided, after reflection upon his state, and for good and sufficient reasons, to move house. The place which he chose as eminently suitable was the ear of a certain elephant.

All that remained to do was to make the move, and quite soon Namouss had installed himself in the large and highly attractive quarters. Time passed. The gnat reared several families of gnatlets, and he sent them out into the world. As the years rolled past, he knew the usual moments of tension and relaxation, the feelings of joy and sorrow, of questing and achievement which are the lot of the gnat wherever he may be found.

The elephant's ear was his home; and, as is always the case, he felt (and the feeling persisted until it became quite permanent) that there was a close connection between his life, his history, his very being and this place. The ear was so warm, so welcoming, so vast, the scene of so many experiences.

Naturally Namouss had not moved into the house without due ceremony and a regard for the proper observances of the situation. On the very first day, just before moving in, he had cried, at the top of his tiny voice, his decision. 'O Elephant!'—he had shouted—'Know that none other than I, Namouss the Gnat, known as Perceptive Namouss, propose to make this place my abode. As it is your ear, I am giving you the customary notice of my intention.'

The elephant had raised no objection.

But Namouss did not know that the elephant had not heard him at all. Neither, for that matter, had his host felt the entry (or even the presence and absence) of the gnat and his various families. Not to labour the point unduly, he had no idea that gnats were there at all.

And when the time came when Namouss the Perceptive decided, for what were to him compelling and important reasons, that he would move house again, he reflected that he must do so in accordance with established and hallowed custom. He prepared himself for the formal declaration of his abandonment of the Elephant's Ear.

Thus it was that, the decision finally and irrevocably taken and his words sufficiently rehearsed, Namouss shouted once more down the elephant's ear. He shouted once, and no answer came. He shouted again, and the elephant was still silent. The third time, gathering the whole strength of his voice in his determination to register his urgent yet eloquent words, he cried: 'O Elephant! Know that I, the Gnat Perceptive Namouss, propose to leave my hearth and home, to quit my residence in this ear of yours where I have dwelt for so very long. And this is for a sufficient and significant reason which I am prepared to explain to you.'

Now finally the words of the gnat came to the hearing of the elephant, and the gnat-cry penetrated. As the elephant pondered the words, Namouss shouted: 'What have you to say in answer to my news? What are your feelings about my departure?'

The elephant raised his great head and trumpeted a little. And this trumpeting contained the sense: 'Go in peace—for in truth your going is of as much interest and significance to me as was your coming.'

తు

The Tale of Perceptive Namouss might be taken at first glance as a sardonic illustration of a supposed uselessness of life. Such an interpretation, the Sufi would say, could only be due to the insensitivity of the reader.

What is intended to be stressed here is the general lack of human judgment about the relative importance of things in life.

Man thinks that important things are unimportant, and that trivial ones are vital.

This story is attributed to Sheikh Hamza Malamati Maqtul. He organized the Malamatis and was executed in 1575, alleged to be a Christian.

The Idiot, the Wise Man and the Jug

AN idiot may be the name given to the ordinary man, who consistently misinterprets what happens to him, what he does, or what is brought about by others. He does this so completely plausibly that—for himself and his peers—large areas of life and thought seem logical and true.

An idiot of this kind was sent one day with a pitcher to a wise man, to collect some wine.

On the way the idiot, through his own heedlessness, smashed the jar against a rock.

When he arrived at the house of the wise man, he presented him with the handle of the pitcher, and said:

'So-and-so sent you this pitcher, but a horrid stone stole it from me.'

Amused and wishing to test his coherence, the wise man asked:

'Since the pitcher is stolen, why do you offer me the handle?'

'I am not such a fool as people say,' the idiot told him, 'and therefore I have brought the handle to prove my story.'

ഇ

A recurrent theme among the dervish teachers is that humanity generally cannot distinguish a hidden trend in events which alone would enable it to make full use of life. Those who can see this thread are termed the Wise; while the ordinary man is said to be 'asleep', or called the Idiot.

This story, quoted in English by Colonel Wilberforce Clarke (*Diwan-i-Hafiz*) is a typical one. The contention is constructive: that by absorbing this doctrine through such caricatures, certain human beings can actually 'sensitize' themselves for the perception of the hidden trend.

The present extract is from a dervish collection attributed to Pir-i-do-Sara, 'The Wearer of the Patchwork Robe', who died in 1790 and is buried at Mazar-i-Sharif in Turkestan.

The Wayward Princess

A CERTAIN king believed that what he had been taught, and what he believed, was right. In many ways he was a just man, but he was one whose ideas were limited.

One day he said to his three daughters:

'All that I have is yours, or will be yours. Through me you obtained your life. It is my will which determines your future, and hence determines your fate.'

Dutifully, and quite persuaded of the truth of this, two of the girls agreed.

The third daughter, however, said:

'Although my position demands that I be obedient to the laws, I cannot believe that my fate must always be determined by your opinions.'

'We shall see about that,' said the king.

He ordered her to be imprisoned in a small cell, where she languished for years. Meanwhile the king and his obedient daughters spent freely of the wealth which would otherwise have been expended upon her.

The king said to himself:

'This girl lies in prison not by her own will, but by mine. This proves, sufficiently for any logical mind, that it is *my* will, not hers, which is determining her fate.'

The people of the country, hearing of their princess's situation, said to one another:

'She must have done or said something very wrong for a monarch, with whom we find no fault, to treat his own flesh and blood so.' For they had not arrived at the point where they felt the need to dispute the king's assumption of rightness in everything.

From time to time the king visited the girl. Although she was pale and weakened from her imprisonment, she refused to change her attitude.

Finally the king's patience came to an end.

'Your continued defiance,' he said to her, 'will only annoy me further, and seem to weaken my rights, if you stay within my realms. I could kill you; but I am merciful. I therefore banish you into the wilderness adjoining my territory. This is a wilderness, inhabited only by wild beasts and such eccentric outcasts who cannot survive in our rational society. There you will soon discover whether you can have an existence apart from that of your family; and, if you can, whether you prefer it to ours.'

His decree was at once obeyed, and she was conveyed to the borders of the kingdom. The princess found herself set loose in a wild land which bore little resemblance to the sheltered surroundings of her upbringing. But she soon learned that a cave would serve for a house, that nuts and fruit came from trees as well as from golden plates, that warmth came from the Sun. This wilderness had a climate and a way of existing of its own.

After some time she had so ordered her life that she had water from springs, vegetables from the earth, fire from a smouldering tree.

'Here,' she said to herself, 'is a life whose elements belong together, form a completeness, yet neither individually nor collectively do they obey the commands of my father the king.'

One day a lost traveller—as it happened a man of great riches and ingenuity—came upon the exiled princess, fell in love with her, and took her back to his own country, where they were married.

After a space of time, the two decided to return to the wilderness where they built a huge and prosperous city where their wisdom. resources and faith were expressed to their fullest possible extent, The 'eccentrics' and other outcasts, many of them thought to be madmen, harmonized completely and usefully with this many-sided life.

The city and its surrounding countryside became renowned throughout the entire world. It was not long before its power and beauty far outshone that of the realm of the princess's father.

By the unanimous choice of the inhabitants, the princess and her husband were elected to the joint monarchy of this new and ideal kingdom.

At length the king decided to visit the strange and mysterious place which had sprung up in a wilderness, and which was, he heard, peopled at least in part by those whom he and his like despised.

As, with bowed head, he slowly approached the foot of the throne upon which the young couple sat and raised his eyes to meet those whose repute of justice, prosperity and understanding far exceeded his own, he was able to catch the murmured words of his daughter:

'You see, Father, every man and woman has his own fate and his own choice.'

ᴥ

Sultan Saladin, according to a Sufi manuscript, met the great teacher Ahmed el-Rifai, founder of the Rifai Order, the 'Howling Dervishes', and asked him several questions.

This story was related by the Rifai in answer to the inquiry: 'What reason, if any, have you for supposing that the imposition of the rule of the Law is insufficient for maintaining happiness and justice?'

The meeting took place in 1174, but the story, which is known in other traditions than the Sufi one, has been used since to illustrate the possibility of 'a different state of consciousness' in man.

The Bequest

A MAN died far from his home, and in the portion of his will which he had available for bequest, he left in these words: 'Let the community where the land is situated take what they wish for themselves, and let them give that which they wish to Arif the Humble.'

Now Arif was a young man at the time, who had far less apparent authority than anyone in the community. Therefore the elders took possession of whatever they wanted from the land which had been left, and they allocated to Arif a few trifles only, which nobody else wanted.

Many years later Arif, grown to strength and wisdom, went to the community to claim his patrimony. 'These are the objects which we have allocated to you in accordance with the Will,' said the elders. They did not feel that they had usurped anything, for they had been told to take what they wished.

But, in the middle of the discussion, an unknown man of grave countenance and compelling presence appeared among them. He said: 'The meaning of the Will was that you should give to Arif that which you wished *for yourselves*, for he can make the best use of it.'

In the moment of illumination which this statement gave them, the elders were able to see the true meaning of the phrase, 'Let them give that which they wish to Arif'.

'Know', continued the apparition, 'that the testator died unable to protect his property, which would, in case of his making Arif his legatee in an obvious sense, have been usurped by this Community. At the very least it would have caused dissension. So he entrusted it to you, knowing that if you thought that it was your own property you would take care of it. Hence he made a wise provision for the preservation and transmission of this treasure. The time has now come for it to be returned to its rightful use.'

Thus it was that the property was handed back; the elders were able to see the truth.

∾

The Sufi teaching that people wish for themselves what they should wish for others is stressed in this story by Sayed Ghaus Ali Shah, the Qadiri Order's saint who died in 1881 and is buried at Panipat.

This idea is not uncommon, though in folklore it is usually interpreted to show how a bequest came in the long run to a deserving legatee who had for years been unable to claim his patrimony.

In some dervish circles this story is taught as an illustration of the claim: 'You have many endowments which are yours on trust alone; when you understand this, you can give them to the rightful owners.'

The Oath

A MAN who was troubled in mind once swore that if his problems were solved he would sell his house and give all the money gained from it to the poor.

The time came when he realized that he must redeem his oath. But he did not want to give away so much money. So he thought of a way out.

He put the house on sale at one silver piece. Included with the house, however, was a cat. The price asked for this animal was ten thousand pieces of silver.

Another man bought the house and cat. The first man gave the single piece of silver to the poor, and pocketed the ten thousand for himself.

Many people's minds work like this. They resolve to follow a teaching; but they interpret their relationship with it to their own advantage. Until they overcome this tendency by special training, they cannot learn at all.

❦

The trick described in this story, according to its dervish teller (Sheikh Nasir el-Din Shah) may be deliberate — or it may describe the warped mind which unconsciously performs tricks of this kind.

The Sheikh, also known as 'The Lamp of Delhi', died in 1846. His shrine is in Delhi, India. This version, attributed to him, is from an oral tradition of the Chishti Order. It is used to introduce the psychological technique designed to stabilize the mind, making it incapable of tricks of self-deception.

The Idiot in the Great City

THERE are different kinds of awakening. Only one is the right way. Man is asleep, but he must wake in the right way. There is a story of an ignoramus whose awakening was not correct:

This idiot came to a huge city, and he was confused by the number of people in the streets. Fearing that if he slept and woke again he would not be able to find himself among so many people, he tied a gourd to his ankle for identification.

A practical joker, knowing what he had done, waited until he was asleep, then removed the gourd and tied it around his own leg. He, too, lay down on the caravanserai floor to sleep. The fool woke first, and saw the gourd. At first he thought that this other man must be him. Then he attacked the other, shouting: 'If you are me: then who, for heaven's sake, who and where am I?'

This tale, which also appears in the Mulla Nasrudin corpus of jokes which is known throughout Central Asia, is preserved in the great spiritual classic *Salaman and Absal*, by the fifteenth-century author and mystic Abdur-Rahman Jami. He came from across the Oxus and died in Herat after establishing himself as one of the greatest literary figures in the Persian language.

Jami caused a great deal of resentment among divines because of his forthrightness, especially by saying that he recognized no teacher except his own father.

The Founding of a Tradition

ONCE upon a time there was a town composed of two parallel streets. A dervish passed through one street into the other, and as he reached the second one, the people there noticed that his eyes were streaming with tears. 'Someone has died in the other street! one cried, and soon all the children in the neighbourhood had taken up the cry.

What had really happened was that the dervish had been peeling onions.

Within a short space of time the cry had reached the first street; and the adults of both streets were so distressed and fearful (for each community was related to the other) that they dared not make complete inquiries as to the cause of the furore.

A wise man tried to reason with the people of both streets, asking why they did not question each other. Too confused to know what they meant, some said: 'For all we know there is a deadly plague in the other street.'

This rumour, too, spread like wildfire, until each street's populace thought that the other was doomed.

When some measure of order was restored, it was only enough for the two communities to decide to emigrate to save themselves. Thus it was that, from different sides of the town, both streets entirely evacuated their people.

Now, centuries later, the town is still deserted; and not so far away are two villages. Each village has its own tradition of how it began as a settlement from a doomed town, through a fortunate flight, in remote times, from a nameless evil.

ॐ

In their psychological teaching, Sufis claim that ordinary transmission of knowledge is subject to so much deformation through editing and false memory that it cannot be taken as a substitute for direct perception of fact.

Illustrating subjectivity of the human brain, 'The Founding of a Tradition' is quoted from the teaching-book *Asrar-i-Khilwatia* ('Secrets of the Recluses') by Sheikh Qalandar Shah, of the Suhrawardi Order, who died in 1832. His shrine is at Lahore, in Pakistan.

Fatima the Spinner and the Tent

ONCE in a city in the Farthest West there lived a girl called Fatima. She was the daughter of a prosperous spinner. One day her father said to her: 'Come, daughter; we are going on a journey, for I have business in the islands of the Middle Sea. Perhaps you may find some handsome youth in a good situation whom you could take as husband.'

They set off and travelled from island to island, the father doing his trading while Fatima dreamt of the husband who might soon be hers. One day, however, they were on the way to Crete when a storm blew up, and the ship was wrecked. Fatima, only half-conscious, was cast up on the seashore near Alexandria. Her father was dead, and she was utterly destitute.

She could only remember dimly her life until then, for her experience of the shipwreck, and her exposure in the sea, had utterly exhausted her.

While she was wandering on the sands, a family of cloth-makers found her. Although they were poor, they took her into their humble home and taught her their craft. Thus it was that she made a second life for herself, and within a year or two she was happy and reconciled to her lot. But one day, when she was on the seashore for some reason, a band of slave-traders landed and carried her, along with other captives, away with them.

Although she bitterly lamented her lot, Fatima found no sympathy from the slavers, who took her to Istanbul and sold her as a slave.

Her world had collapsed for the second time. Now it chanced that there were few buyers at the market. One of them was a man who was looking for slaves to work in his woodyard, where he made masts for ships. When he saw the dejection of the unfortunate Fatima, he decided to buy her, thinking that in this way, at least, he might be able to give her a slightly better life than if she were bought by someone else.

He took Fatima to his home, intending to make her a serving-maid for his wife. When he arrived at the house, however, he found that he had lost all his money in a cargo which had been captured by pirates. He could not afford workers, so he, Fatima and his wife were left alone to work at the heavy labour of making masts.

Fatima, grateful to her employer for rescuing her, worked so hard and so well that he gave her her freedom, and she became his trusted helper. Thus it was that she became comparatively happy in her third career.

One day he said to her: 'Fatima, I want you to go with a cargo of ships' masts to Java, as my agent, and be sure that you sell them at a profit.'

She set off, but when the ship was off the coast of China a typhoon wrecked it, and Fatima found herself again cast up on the seashore of a strange land. Once again she wept bitterly, for she felt that nothing in her life was working in accordance with expectation. Whenever things seemed to be going well, something came and destroyed all her hopes.

'Why is it', she cried out, for the third time, 'that whenever I try to do something it comes to grief? Why should so many unfortunate things happen to me?' But there was no answer. So she picked herself up from the sand, and started to walk inland.

Now it so happened that nobody in China had heard of Fatima, or knew anything about her troubles. But there was a legend that a certain stranger, a woman, would one day arrive there, and that she would be able to make a tent for the Emperor. And, since there was as yet nobody in China who could make tents, everyone looked upon the fulfilment of this prediction with the liveliest anticipation.

In order to make sure that this stranger, when she arrived, would not be missed, successive Emperors of China had followed the custom of sending heralds, once a year, to all the towns and villages of the land, asking for any foreign woman to be produced at Court.

When Fatima stumbled into a town by the Chinese seashore, it was one such occasion. The people spoke to her through an interpreter, and explained that she would have to go to see the Emperor.

'Lady,' said the Emperor, when Fatima was brought before him, 'can you make a tent?'

'I think so,' said Fatima.

She asked for rope, but there was none to be had. So, remembering her time as a spinner, she collected flax and made ropes. Then she asked for stout cloth, but the Chinese had none of the kind which she needed. So, drawing on her experience with the weavers of Alexandria, she made some stout tentcloth. Then she found that she needed tent-poles, but there were none in China. So Fatima, remembering how she had been trained by the wood-fashioner of Istanbul, cunningly made stout tent-poles. When these were ready, she racked her brains for the memory of all the tents she had seen in her travels: and lo, a tent was made.

When this wonder was revealed to the Emperor of China, he offered Fatima the fulfilment of any wish she cared to name. She chose to settle in China, where she married a handsome prince, and where she remained in happiness, surrounded by her children, until the end of her days.

It was through these adventures that Fatima realized that what had appeared to be an unpleasant experience at the time, turned out to be an essential part of the making of her ultimate happiness.

∞

This story is well known in Greek folklore, many of whose contemporary motifs feature dervishes and their legends. The version cited here is attributed to the Sheikh Mohamed Jamaludin of Adrianople. He founded the Jamalia Order ('The Beautiful'), and died in 1750.

The Gates of Paradise

ଛ୍ୟାଛ୍ୟାଛ୍ୟାଛ୍ୟାଛ୍ୟାଛ୍ୟାଛ୍ୟାଛ୍ୟାଛ୍ୟାଛ୍ୟାଛ୍ୟାଛ୍ୟାଛ୍ୟାଛ୍ୟାଛ୍ୟାଛ୍ୟାଛ୍ୟାଛ୍ୟାଛ୍ୟା

THERE was once a good man. He had spent his whole life in culti-
vating the qualities enjoined upon those who would reach Paradise. He gave freely to the poor, he loved his fellow creatures and he
served them. Remembering the need to have patience, he endured
great and unexpected hardships, often for the sake of others. He
made journeys in search of knowledge. His humility and exemplary
behaviour were such that his repute as a wise man and good citizen
resounded from the East to the West, and from the North to the
South.

All these qualities he did indeed exercise—whenever he remembered to do so. But he had one shortcoming, and that was heedlessness. This tendency was not strong in him, and he considered
that, balanced against the other things which he did practise, it
could only be regarded as a small fault. There were some poor
people whom he did not help, because from time to time he was
insensitive to their needs. Love and service, too, were sometimes
forgotten when what he thought to be personal needs, or at least
desires, welled up in him.

He was fond of sleep; and sometimes when he was asleep, opportunities to seek knowledge, or to understand it, or to practise real
humility, or to add to the sum total of good behaviour—such
opportunities passed by, and they did not return.

Just as the good qualities left their impress upon his essential self,
so did the characteristic of heedlessness.

And then he died. Finding himself beyond this life, and making
his way towards the doors of the Walled Garden, the man paused,
to examine his conscience. And he felt that his opportunity of
entering the High Portals was enough.

The gates, he saw, were shut; and then a voice addressed him,
saying: 'Be watchful; for the gates will open only once in every

75

hundred years.' He settled down to wait, excited at the prospect. But, deprived of chances to exercise virtues towards mankind, he found that his capacity of attention was not enough for him. After watching for what seemed like an age, his head nodded in sleep. For an instant his eyelids closed. And in that infinitesimal moment the gates yawned open. Before his eyes were fully open again, they closed: with a roar loud enough to wake the dead.

※

This is a favourite dervish teaching, sometimes called 'The Parable of Heedlessness'. Although well known as a folk-tale, its origins are lost. Some have attributed it to Hadrat Ali, the Fourth Caliph. Others say that it was so important as to be passed down, secretly, from the Prophet himself. It certainly is not to be found in any of the attested Traditions of the Prophet.

The literary form in which it is given here derives from the works of an unknown dervish of the seventeenth century, Amil-Baba, whose manuscripts stress that 'the real author is him whose work is anonymous, for in that way nobody stands between the learner and that which is learned.'

The Man Who Was Aware of Death

THERE was once a dervish who embarked upon a sea journey. As the other passengers in the ship came aboard one by one, they saw him and — as is the custom — asked him for a piece of advice. All the dervish would do was to say the same thing to each one of them: he seemed merely to be repeating one of those formula which each dervish makes the object of his attention from time to time.

The formula was: 'Try to be aware of death, until you know what death is.' Few of the travellers felt particularly attracted to this admonition.

Presently a terrible storm blew up. The crew and the passengers alike fell upon their knees, imploring God to save the ship. They alternately screamed in terror, gave themselves up for lost, hoped wildly for succour. All this time the dervish sat quietly, reflective, reacting not at all to the movement and the scenes which surrounded him.

Eventually the buffeting stopped, the sea and sky were calm, and the passengers became aware how serene the dervish had been throughout the episode.

One of them asked him: 'Did you not realize that during this frightful tempest there was nothing more solid than a plank between us all and death?'

'Oh, yes, indeed,' answered the dervish. 'I knew that at sea it is always thus. I also realized, however, that I had often reflected when I was on land that, in the normal course of events, there is *even less* between us and death.'

ന്ദ

The Man Who Was Aware of Death

This story is by Bayazid of Bistam, a place to the south of the Caspian Sea. He was one of the greatest of the ancient Sufis, and died in the latter part of the ninth century.

His grandfather was a Zoroastrian, and he received his esoteric training in India. Because his master, Abu-Ali of Sind, did not know the external rituals of Islam perfectly, some scholars have assumed that Abu-Ali was a Hindu, and that Bayazid was in fact studying Indian mystical methods. No responsible authority, however, accords with this view, among the Sufis. The followers of Bayazid include the Bistamia Order.

The Man Who Was Easily Angered

೫ಲ

A MAN who was very easily angered realized after many years that all his life he had been in difficulties because of this tendency.

One day he heard of a dervish deep of knowledge, whom he went to see, asking for advice.

The dervish said: 'Go to such-and-such a crossroads. There you will find a withered tree. Stand under it and offer water to every traveller who passes that place.'

The man did as he was told. Many days passed, and he became well known as one who was following a certain discipline of charity and self-control, under the instructions of a man of real knowledge.

One day a man in a hurry turned his head away when he was offered the water, and went on walking along the road. The man who was easily angered called out to him several times: 'Come, return my salutation! Have some of this water, which I provide for all travellers!'

But there was no reply.

Overcome by this behaviour, the first man forgot his discipline completely. He reached for his gun, which was hooked in the withered tree, took aim at the heedless traveller, and fired. The man fell dead.

At the very moment that the bullet entered his body, the withered tree, as if by a miracle, burst joyfully into blossom.

The man who had been killed was a murderer, on his way to commit the worst crime of a long career.

There are, you see, two kinds of advisers. The first kind is the one who tells what should be done according to certain fixed principles, repeated mechanically. The other kind is the Man of Knowledge. Those who meet the Man of Knowledge will ask him for moralistic advice, and will treat him as a moralist. But what he serves is Truth, not pious hopes.

ರಾಣ

The dervish master who figures in this tale is said to have been Najmudin Kubra, one of the greatest of Sufi saints. He founded the Kubravi ('Greater Brethren') which greatly resembled the Order later established by St Francis. Like the Saint of Assisi, Najmudin was reputed to have an uncanny power over animals.

Najmudin was one of the six hundred thousand people who died when Khwarizm in Central Asia was destroyed in 1221. It is stated that the Great Mongol Genghiz Khan, aware of his reputation, offered to spare him if he gave himself up, but he went out with the defenders of the city and was later identified among the dead.

Having foreseen the catastrophe, Najmudin had sent all his disciples away to safety some time before the appearance of the Mongol hordes.

The Dog and the Donkey

A MAN who had found out how to understand the significance of the sounds made by animals, was walking along a village street one day.

He saw a donkey, which had just brayed, and beside him was a dog, yapping away for all he was worth.

As he drew near, the meaning of this exchange came to him.

'All this talk of grass and pastures, when I am waiting for you to say something about rabbits and bones: it bores me,' said the dog.

The man could not restrain bimself. 'There is, however, a central fact—the use of hay, which is like the function of meat,' he objected.

The two animals turned upon him in an instant. The dog barked fiercely to drown his words: and the donkey knocked him senseless with a well-aimed kick of his hind legs.

Then they went back to their argument.

ಬಿ

This story, which resembles one of Rumi's, is a fable from the famed collection of Majnun Qalandar, who wandered for forty years in the thirteenth century, reciting teaching-stories in market-places. Some said that he was completely mad (which is what his name means); others that he was one of the 'Changed Ones'—who have developed a sense of the relationship between things which the ordinary person thinks to be separate.

Carrying Shoes

Two pious and worthy men went into a mosque together. The first one took off his shoes and placed them neatly, side by side, outside the door. The second man removed his shoes, placed them sole to sole and took them into the mosque with him.

There was an argument among a group of other pious and worthy folk who were sitting at the door, as to which of these men was the better. 'If one went barefoot into a mosque, was it not better to leave the very shoes outside?' asked one. 'But should we not consider', said another, 'that the man who took his shoes into the mosque carried them to remind himself by their very presence that he was in a state of proper humility?'

When the two men came out after their prayers, they were questioned separately, as it happened, by different parties from the onlookers.

The first man said: 'I left my shoes outside for the usual reason The reason is that if anyone wants to steal them he will have an opportunity of resisting that temptation, and thus acquiring merit for himself.' The listeners were most impressed by the high-mindedness of a man whose possessions were of so little account to him that he willingly entrusted them to whatever might be their fate.

The second man, at the same time, was saying: 'I took my shoes into the mosque because, had I left them outside, they might have constituted a temptation to steal them. Whoever had yielded to this temptation would have made me his accomplice in sin.' The hearers were most impressed by this pious sentiment, and admired the thoughtfulness of the sage.

But yet another man, a man of wisdom, who was present, cried out: 'While you two men and your followers have been indulging in your admirable sentiment, training each other with the play of hypothetical instances, certain *real* things have been happening.'

'What were these things?' asked the crowd.

'Nobody was tempted by the shoes. Nobody was not tempted by the shoes. The theoretical sinner did not pass by. Instead, another man altogether, who had no shoes at all to carry with him or to leave outside, entered the mosque. Nobody noticed his conduct. He was not conscious of the effect which he might be having on people who saw him or did not see him. But, because of his real sincerity, his prayers in this mosque today helped, in the most direct way possible, all the potential thieves who might or might not steal shoes or reform themselves by being exposed to temptation.'

Do you still not see that the mere practice of self-conscious conduct, however excellent in its own realm, is a pale thing indeed when measured against the knowledge that there are real men of wisdom?

တတ

This tale, from the teachings of the Khilwati ('recluse') Order, founded by Omar Khilwati who died in 1397, is often quoted. The argument, a common one among dervishes, insists that those who have developed certain inner qualities have a far greater effect upon society than those who try to act on moral principles alone. The former are called: 'The real men of action'; and the latter: 'Those who do not know but play at knowing.'

The Man Who Walked on Water

A CONVENTIONALLY-MINDED dervish, from an austerely pious school, was walking one day along a river bank. He was absorbed in concentration upon moralistic and scholastic problems, for this was the form which Sufi teaching had taken in the community to which he belonged. He equated emotional religion with the search for ultimate Truth.

Suddenly his thoughts were interrupted by a loud shout: someone was repeating the dervish call. 'There is no point in that,' he said to himself, 'because the man is mispronouncing the syllables. Instead of intoning YA HU, he is saying U YA HU.'

Then he realized that he had a duty, as a more careful student, to correct this unfortunate person, who might have had no opportunity of being rightly guided, and was therefore probably only doing his best to attune himself with the idea behind the sounds.

So he hired a boat and made his way to the island in midstream from which the sound appeared to come.

Sitting in a reed hut he found a man, dressed in a dervish robe, moving in time to his own repetition of the initiatory phrase. 'My friend,' said the first dervish, 'you are mispronouncing the phrase. It is incumbent upon me to tell you this, because there is merit for him who gives and him who takes advice. This is the way in which you speak it.' And he told him.

'Thank you,' said the other dervish humbly.

The first dervish entered his boat again, full of satisfaction at having done a good deed. After all, it was said that a man who could repeat the sacred formula correctly could even walk upon the waves: something that he had never seen, but always hoped—for some reason—to be able to achieve.

Now he could hear nothing from the reed hut, but he was sure that his lesson had been well taken.

Then he heard a faltering U YA as the second dervish started to repeat the phrase in his old way ...

While the first dervish was thinking about this, reflecting upon the perversity of humanity and its persistence in error, he suddenly saw a strange sight. From the island the other dervish was coming towards him, walking on the surface of the water ...

Amazed, he stopped rowing. The second dervish walked up to him and said: 'Brother, I am sorry to trouble you, but I have to come out to ask you again the standard method of making the repetition you were telling me, because I find it difficult to remember it.'

৷৹৻৹

In English we can reproduce only one of the ranges of significance of this tale, because the Arabic versions generally make use of words of similar sound with different meanings — homonyms — to signpost the claim that this is an artifact designed to draw the consciousness deeper, as well as something with a superficial moral.

In addition to figuring in popular current literature in the East, the story is found in dervish teaching manuscripts, some of very great age.

This version is from the Asaaseen ('essential', 'original') Order, of the Near and Middle East.

The Ant and the Dragonfly

AN ANT with a settled programme in its mind was looking at some nectar when a dragonfly swooped to taste from the flower's cup. It flitted away and came and swooped again.

This time the ant said:

'You live without labour, and you have no plan. As you have no real nor comparative purpose, what is the dominant feature of your life—and where will it end?'

Said the dragonfly:

'I am happy, and I seek pleasure, this is existence and objective enough. My aim is to have no aim. You may plan as you will; you cannot convince me that there is anything better. You to your plan, me to mine.'

The ant thought:

'That which is visible to me is invisible to him. He does know what happens to ants. I know what happens to dragonflies. Him to his plan, I to mine.'

And the ant went his way, for he had admonished as far as was possible in the circumstances.

Some time later their paths crossed again.

The ant had found a butcher's shop, and he was standing under the chopping-block with discretion, awaiting what would come to him.

The dragonfly, seeing the red meat from above, came gliding down and settled on it. At that moment the butcher's cleaver descended and cut the dragonfly in two.

One half of the body rolled on to the floor at the feet of the ant. Taking up the corpse and starting to drag it towards his nest, the ant recited to himself:

'His plan is finished, and mine continues. "He to his plan" is ended, "Me to mine" begins a cycle. Pride seemed important, it was

a transitory thing. A life of eating, to end with being eaten by
something else. When I suggested this, all he could think was that
I might be a killjoy.'

∞

Almost the same tale is found in Attar's *Divine Book*, although
the application is slightly different from this version, which
was related by a Bokharan dervish near the tomb of El-Shah,
Bahaudin Naqshband, sixty years ago. It is from a Sufi notebook kept in the Great Mosque of Jalalabad.

The Story of Tea

In ancient times, tea was not known outside China. Rumours of its existence had reached the wise and the unwise of other countries, and each tried to find out what it was in accordance with what he wanted or what he thought it should be.

The King of Inja ('here') sent an embassy to China, and they were given tea by the Chinese Emperor. But, since they saw that the peasants drank it too, they concluded that it was not fit for their royal master: and, furthermore, that the Chinese Emperor was trying to deceive them, passing off some other substance for the celestial drink.

The greatest philosopher of Anja ('there') collected all the information he could about tea, and concluded that it must be a substance which existed but rarely, and was of another order than anything then known. For was it not referred to as being a herb, a water, green, black, sometimes bitter, sometimes sweet?

In the countries of Koshish and Bebinem, for centuries the people tested all the herbs they could find. Many were poisoned, all were disappointed. For nobody had brought the tea-plant to their lands, and thus they could not find it. They also drank all the liquids which they could find, but to no avail.

In the territory of Mazhab ('Sectarianism') a small bag of tea was carried in procession before the people as they went on their religious observances. Nobody thought of tasting it: indeed, nobody knew how. All were convinced that the tea itself had a magical quality. A wise man said: 'Pour upon it boiling water, ye ignorant ones!' They hanged him and nailed him up, because to do this, according to their belief, would mean the destruction of their tea. This showed that he was an enemy of their religion.

Before he died, he had told his secret to a few, and they managed to obtain some tea and drink it secretly. When anyone said: 'What are you doing?' they answered: 'It is but medicine which we take for a certain disease.'

And so it was throughout the world. Tea had actually been seen growing by some, who did not recognize it. It had been given to others to drink, but they thought it the beverage of the common people. It had been in the possession of others, and they worshipped it. Outside China, only a few people actually drank it, and those covertly.

Then came a man of knowledge, who said to the merchants of tea, and the drinkers of tea, and to others: 'He who tastes, knows. He who tastes not, knows not. Instead of talking about the celestial beverage, say nothing, but offer it at your banquets. Those who like it will ask for more. Those who do not, will show that they are not fitted to be tea-drinkers. Close the shop of argument and mystery. Open the teahouse of experience.'

The tea was brought from one stage to another along the Silk Road, and whenever a merchant carrying jade or gems or silk would pause to rest, he would make tea, and offer it to such people as were near him, whether they were aware of the repute of tea or not. This was the beginning of the Chaikhanas, the teahouses which were established all the way from Peking to Bokhara and Samarkand. And those who tasted, knew.

At first, mark well, it was only the great and the pretended men of wisdom who sought the celestial drink and who also exclaimed: 'But this is only dried leaves!' or: 'Why do you boil water, stranger, when all I want is the celestial drink?', or yet again: 'How do I know what this is? Prove it to me. Besides the colour of the liquid is not golden, but ochre!'

When the truth was known, and when the tea was brought for all who would taste, the roles were reversed, and the only people who said things like the great and intelligent had said were the absolute fools. And such is the case to this day.

໖໖

89

ɷ

The Story of Tea

Drinks of all kinds have been used by almost all peoples as allegories connected with the search for higher knowledge.

Coffee, the most recent of social drinks, was discovered by the dervish sheikh Abu el-Hasan Shadhili, at Mocha in Arabia.

Although the Sufis and others often clearly state that 'magical drinks' (wine, the water of life) are an analogy of a certain experience, literalist students tend to believe that the origin of these myths dates from the discovery of some hallucinogenic or inebrietive quality in potations. According to the dervishes, such an idea is a reflection of the investigator's incapacity to understand that they are speaking in parallels.

This tale is from the teachings of the Master Hamadani (died 1140) teacher of the great Yasavi of Turkestan.

The King Who Decided to be Generous

THERE was a king of Iran who said to a dervish: 'Tell me a story.'

The dervish said: 'Your Majesty, I will tell you the tale of Hatim Tai, the Arabian King and the most generous man of all time; for if you could be like him, you would indeed be the greatest king alive.'

'Speak on,' said the king, 'but if you do not please me, having cast aspersions upon my generosity, you will lose your head.' He talked in this way because in Persia it is customary for those at Court to tell the monarch that he already has the most excellent qualities of anyone in the world; past, present or future.

'To continue,' said the dervish, in the manner of dervishes (for they are not easily discountenanced), 'Hatim Tai's generosity excelled, in letter and spirit, that of all other men.' And this is the story which the dervish told.

Another Arabian king coveted the possessions, the villages and oases, the camels and the fighting-men of Hatim Tai. So this man declared war upon Hatim, sending him a messenger with the declaration of war: 'Yield to me, otherwise I shall surely overrun you and your lands, and possess myself of your sovereignty.'

When this message reached Hatim's court, his advisers at once suggested that he mobilize the warriors in defence of his realm saying: 'There is surely not an able-bodied man or woman among your followers who will not gladly lay down his life in defence of our beloved king.'

But Hatim, contrary to the expectation of the people, said:

'No, instead of your riding forth and shedding your blood for me, I shall flee. It would be far from the path of generosity if I were to become the cause of the sacrifice of a life of a single man or woman. If you yield peaceably, this king will content himself with

91

taking only your services and rents, and you will have suffered no material loss. If, on the other hand, you resist, by the conventions of war he will be entitled to regard your possessions as booty, and if you lose the war you will be penniless.'

So saying, Hatim took only a stout staff and went into the near-by mountains, where he found a cave and sank himself in contemplation.

Half of the people were deeply affected by this sacrifice of his wealth and position by Hatim Tai on their behalf. But others, especially those who sought to make a name for themselves on the field of valour, muttered: 'How do we know that this man is not a simple coward?' And others, who had little courage, muttered against him saying: 'He has, in a sense, saved himself; for he has abandoned us to a fate which is unknown to us. Perhaps we may become the slaves of this unknown king who is, after all, enough of a tyrant to declare war upon his neighbours.'

Others again, uncertain as to what to believe, remained silent, until they should have some means of making up their minds.

And so it was that the tyrant king, accompanied by his glittering hosts, took possession of Hatim Tai's domain. He did not increase the taxes, he did not usurp for himself more than Hatim had taken from the people in exchange for being their protector and administrator of justice. But one thing disturbed him. It was the fact that he heard whispers that, although he had possessed himself of a new realm, yet it had been yielded up to him as an act of generosity by Hatim Tai. These were the words spoken by some of the people.

'I cannot be real master of this land,' declared the tyrant, 'until I have captured Hatim Tai himself. While he lives, there is still a loyalty towards him in the hearts of some of these people. This means that they are not completely my subjects, even though they behave outwardly as such.'

So he published an edict that whoever should bring him Hatim Tai would be rewarded with five thousand pieces of gold. Hatim Tai knew nothing of this until one day he was sitting outside his cave and he heard a conversation between a woodcutter and his wife.

The woodcutter said: 'My dear wife, I am now old and you are much younger than I. We have small children, and in the natural order of events I may be expected to die before you and while the children are youngsters. If we could only find and capture Hatim Tai, for whom there is a reward of five thousand pieces of gold from the new king, your future would be secure.'

'Shame on you!' said his wife. 'Better that you should die, and that I and our children should starve, than that our hands should be stained with the blood of the most generous man of all time, who sacrificed all for our sake.'

'That is all very well,' said the old man, 'but a man has to think of his own interests. I have, after all, responsibilities. And, in any case, every day more and more people believe that Hatim is a coward. It will only be a matter of time before they have searched every possible piece of cover for him.'

'The belief in Hatim's cowardice is fuelled by love of gold. Much more of this kind of talk and Hatim will have lived in vain.'

At that moment Hatim Tai stood up and revealed himself to the astonished pair. 'I am Hatim Tai,' he said. 'Take me to the new king and claim your reward.'

The old man was ashamed, and his eyes filled with tears. 'No, great Hatim,' he said, 'I cannot bring myself to do it.'

While they were arguing, a number of people, who had been searching for the fugitive king, gathered around.

'Unless you do so,' said Hatim, 'I will surrender myself to the king and tell him that you have been hiding me. In that case, you will be executed for treason.'

Realizing that this was Hatim, the mob moved forward, seized their former king, and carried him to the tyrant, with the wood-cutter following miserably behind.

When they got to the court, each claimed that he had himself captured Hatim. The former king, seeing irresolution on the face of his successor, asked to be allowed to speak: 'Know, O King, that my evidence should also be heard. I was captured by this old wood-cutter and not by yonder mob. Give him, therefore, his reward, and do what you will with me ... '

At this the woodcutter stepped forward and told the king the truth about Hatim's having offered himself as a sacrifice for the future security of his family.

The new king was so overwhelmed by this story that he ordered his army to withdraw, placed Hatim Tai back on his throne, and retired to his own country.

When he had heard this story, the king of Iran, forgetting his threat against the dervish, said: 'An excellent tale, O dervish, and one from which we can benefit. You, at any rate, cannot benefit, having abandoned already your expectations of this life and being possessed of nothing. But I, I am a king. And I am rich. Arab kings, people who live on boiled lizards, cannot match a Persian when it comes to real generosity. An idea strikes me! Let us to work!'

Taking the dervish with him, the king of Iran summoned his greatest architects to a large open space and ordered them to design and build an immense palace. It was to be composed of a central strongroom and forty windows.

When it was completed the king caused every available means of transport to be assembled and the palace to be filled with pieces of gold. After months of this activity, a proclamation went forth:

'Lo, the King of Kings, Fountain of Generosity, has ordained that a palace with forty windows be constructed. He will personally, every day, dispense gold to all needy people, from these windows.'

Not unnaturally, large crowds of necessitous ones collected and the king handed out one gold piece to every applicant, appearing at one window each day. Then he noticed that there was a certain dervish who presented himself every day at the window, took his piece of gold and went away. At first the king thought: 'Perhaps he wants to carry the gold to someone who is in need.' Then, when he saw the man again, he thought: 'Perhaps he is applying the dervish rule of secret charity, and redistributes the gold.' And every day when he saw the dervish, he excused him in his own mind, until the fortieth day when the king found that his patience could not endure further. Seizing the hand of the dervish, he said: 'Ungrateful wretch! You neither say "Thank you" nor do you show any esteem for me. You do not smile, you do not bow, you come back day after day. How long can this process continue? Are you saving up from my bounty to become rich, or are you lending out the gold on interest? Far indeed are you from the behaviour of those with the honourable badge of the patched robe.'

As soon as these words had been said, the dervish threw down the forty pieces of gold which he had received. He said to the king: 'Know, O King of Iran, that generosity cannot exist without three things preceding it. The first is giving without the sentiment of generosity; the second is patience; the third is having no suspicions.'

But the king never learned. To him, generosity was bound up with what people would think of him, and how he felt about being 'generous'.

လာ

This traditional story, which is known to readers mainly through the Urdu classic, *The Tale of the Four Dervishes*, succinctly illustrates important Sufi teachings.

Emulation without the basic qualities to sustain that emulation is useless. Generosity cannot be exercised unless other virtues are developed as well.

Some people cannot learn even from exposure to teachings, the latter being represented in the tale by the first and second dervishes.

The Cure of Human Blood

Maulana Bahaudin Naqshband was asked: 'How is it that ignoble men or infants, as in so many stories, can be spiritualized by a glance, or in some indirect way, merely by coming into contact with a great teacher?'

He gave the following story as a reply, saying that this method paralleled the indirect route of spiritualization.

In the days of the great empire of Byzantium, one of its emperors was sick with a dreadful disease, which no doctor could cure. He sent ambassadors to every country with full descriptions of the ailment. One arrived at the school of the great El-Ghazali, who was a Sufi whom the Emperor had only heard of as one of the great sages of the East. El-Ghazali asked one of his disciples to make the journey to Constantinople.

When the man, El-Arif, arrived, he was taken to the Court and treated with all honour, the Emperor beseeching him to effect a cure. Sheikh El-Arif asked what remedies had been tried, and which further ones were contemplated. Then he made an examination of the patient.

Finally he asked for a full audience of all the Court to be called, while he made his declaration of how the cure might be effected.

When all the nobles of the Empire had assembled the Sufi said: 'Your Imperial Majesty had better use faith.'

'The Emperor has faith,' answered a cleric, 'but it does not take therapeutic effect.'

'In that case,' said the Sufi, 'I am compelled to say that there is only one remedy on earth which will save him. But I do not want to speak it, so dreadful a thing is it.'

But he was pressed, promised riches, threatened and cajoled. So he said:

'A bath in the blood of several hundred children under seven years of age will cure the Emperor.'

When the confusion and alarm occasioned by these words had subsided, the Counsellors of State decided that the remedy was worth trying. Some, it is true, said that nobody had any right to attempt such a barbarity at the behest of a foreigner of doubtful origins. The majority, however, considered that any risk was to be taken to preserve the life of an Emperor such as this, whom they all respected and almost worshipped.

They prevailed upon the monarch, in spite of his reluctance, saying: 'Your Imperial Majesty has no right to refuse; for this would deprive his Empire of even more than the life of all his subjects, let alone a number of children.'

Therefore the word was sent around that all children in Byzantium of the required age were to be sent to Constantinople within a certain period, in order to be sacrificed for the Emperor's health.

The mothers of these children in almost every case called down curses upon the head of their ruler, for being such a monster as to demand their flesh and blood for his own salvation. Some, however, prayed instead that the Emperor might be healed before the time set for the slaying of their children.

The Emperor himself, after a certain amount of time had elapsed, began to feel that he could not allow such a deed as the slaughter of young children, on any pretext whatever. The problem put him into such a state of mind that it tortured him night and day; until he gave out the edict: 'I would rather die myself than see the innocent die.'

No sooner had he said this than his sickness began to abate, and he was soon perfectly well again. Shallow thinkers at once concluded that he had been rewarded for his good action. Others, as shallow, attributed his improvement to the relief of the mothers of the children, acting upon Divine power.

When the Sufi El-Arif was asked as to the means by which the disease had abated, he said: 'As he had no faith, he had to have something equivalent to it. This was his single-mindedness coupled with the constructive desires of the mothers who wanted a remission of the disease before a certain time.'

And the scoffers among the Byzantines said: 'What a special dispensation of Divinity it was that the Emperor was healed in response to the holy prayers of the clergy, before the bloodthirsty Saracen's formula was tried. For was it not obvious that he was only trying to destroy the flower of our youth, which would otherwise grow up, and would one day fight against his kind?'

When the matter was reported to El-Ghazali, he said: 'An effect can take place only through a manner devised to operate within the time allotted to its attainment.'

Just as the Sufi leech had to adapt his method to the people with whom he found himself surrounded, so the dervish spiritualizer can activate the inner cognitions of the infant, or the ignoble, even, in the realm of the science of Truth, by the employment of the methods known to him, given to him for this purpose. This latter was the explanation of Our Master Bahaudin.

ನಞ

Khwaja Bahaudin became head of the Order of the Masters (Khwajagan) of Central Asia in the fourteenth century. His surname—which means 'Designer'—was adopted as the title of the School.

Bahaudin of Bokhara is said to have reformed the teachings of the Masters, aligning practice with current needs and collecting vestiges of the tradition from its roots.

He spent seven years as a courtier, seven looking after animals, and seven in road-building before he became a teaching master. His own teacher was the great Baba el-Samasi.

Pilgrims were attracted to Bahaudin's teaching centre from 'the other end of China'. The members of the Order, spread throughout the Turkish and Indian empires and even to Europe and Africa, wore no special robes, and less is known about them than any other Order. Bahaudin was known as El-Shah. Some of the greatest Persian classical poets were

Naqshbandis. Important Naqshbandi books are *The Teachings of El-Shah*, *Secrets of the Naqshbandi Path*, and *Tricklings from the Fountain of Life*. They are to be found only in manuscript form.

Maulana ('Our Master') Bahaudin was born two miles from Bokhara, and is buried near there at Qasr-i-Arifin, the Fortress of the Knowers.

This tale, elicited in response to a question, is from *What Our Master Said*, also called *Teachings of The Shah*.

The Dam

A WIDOW and her five small sons once lived on a piece of irrigated land whose crops gave them a bare living. Their rights to take enough water had been usurped by a tyrant who had barred and locked the channel which could have brought plenty to the family. The eldest brother tried many times to remove the barrier, but he was not strong enough alone—and his younger brothers were only children. Besides, he knew that the tyrant could always restore the dam, so his efforts were more heroic than practical.

One day his father seemed to appear to him in a vision. He gave him certain instructions, instructions of hope. Soon afterwards the villain, angered at the independent behaviour of the youth, declared him a troublemaker throughout the land, and made people feel hostility towards him.

This young man went away to a far city, where he worked for many years as the assistant to a merchant. From time to time he sent home such sums of money as he could, through the hands of travelling merchants. Because he did not want them to feel any obligation, and because it was safer for the merchants themselves not to help people under a cloud, he told them to give the money supposedly in exchange for small services which his brothers could be asked to perform.

After many years, the time came for the elder brother to return. When he arrived home and showed himself, only one brother recognized him, and even he was not quite sure, for he was so much older.

'My elder brother had black hair,' said the younger.

'But I am older now,' said the elder.

'We are no merchants,' said another brother. 'How can this man, dressed as he is and speaking as he does, be one of us?'

The reason was explained to him, but he was not completely convinced.

'I remember how you four were often in my charge, and how you longed for the gushing water trapped beyond the dam,' said the elder brother.

'We do not remember it,' they said, because time had made them almost oblivious to their condition.

'But I sent you gifts, upon which you have mainly lived since the water finally dried up,' said the eldest.

'We know of no gifts; we have had only money we have earned by our own service to sundry travellers,' they all replied together.

'Describe our mother to us,' asked one, still looking for proof.

But since the lady had died so long ago, and their memories had become blurred, all found points to dispute in their brother's description.

'Well, even if you really are our brother, what have you come to say?' they asked.

'That the tyrant is dead. That his soldiers have deserted and have gone to seek other masters, who keep them occupied. That the time is here for us all together to restore greenness and happiness to the land.'

'I remember no tyrant,' said the first brother.

'The land is always like this,' said the second.

'Why should we do as *you* say?' asked the third.

'I would like to help you, but I do not really understand what you are talking about,' said the fourth.

'Besides,' said the first brother, 'I need no water. I collect brushwood and it makes a fire for me. Merchants stop by the fire, and pay me for errands.'

'And', said the second brother, 'water here would only inundate the small pool in which I keep my ornamental carp. Sometimes merchants stop to admire them, and give me tips.'

'For my part,' said the third brother, 'I would like water, but I do not know whether it could restore this land.'

The fourth said nothing at all.

'Let us to work' said the eldest brother.

'Let us rather wait until we see whether the merchants come,' said the others.

'Of course they will not,' said the eldest, 'for I sent them in the first place.'

But they argued, and they argued, and they argued.

This was not the season for the merchants to pass that way, for snow had blocked the passes leading to the brothers' land, as was usual at that time.

Before the season for the caravans along the Silk Road, a second tyrant, worse than the first, made his appearance. Since he was not yet sure of himself as a usurper, he was taking only abandoned lands. He saw the dam, its abandoned state made his covetousness worse, made it grow within him, and he not only took possession of it but also decided to enslave the brothers when he was strong enough, for they were all able-bodied men, even the oldest.

And the brothers are still arguing. It is very unlikely that anything will stop the tyrant now.

ରଣ

Traced to Abu-Ali Mohammed, son of el-Qasim el-Rudbari, this is a famous story of the Path of the Masters, the Tariqa-i-Khwajagan.

It illustrates the mysterious origins of Sufi teachings, which come from one place, yet may seem to come from another: because the human mind cannot perceive (like the brothers in the fable) the 'real Source'.

Rudbari traced his 'Chain of Succession' of teaching from all the ancients among the Sufis, particularly from Shibli, Bayazid, and Hamdun Qassar.

The Three Dervishes

ONCE upon a time there were three dervishes. They were called Yak, Do and Se. They came from the North, the West and the South, respectively. They had one thing in common: they were looking for the Deep Truth, and they sought a Way.

The first, Yak-Baba, sat down and contemplated until his head was sore. The second, Do-Agha, stood on his head until his feet ached. The third, Se-Kalandar, read books until his nose bled.

Finally they decided upon a common effort. They went into retirement and carried out their exercises in unison, hoping by that means to summon enough effort to produce the appearance of Truth, which they called Deep Truth.

For forty days and forty nights they persevered. At last in a whirl of white smoke the head of a very old man appeared, as if from the ground, in front of them. 'Are you the mysterious Khidr, guide of men?' asked the first. 'No, he is the Qutub, the Pillar of the Universe,' said the second. 'I am convinced that this is none other than one of the Abdals, The Changed Ones,' said the third.

'I am none of these,' roared the apparition, 'but I am that which you may think me to be. Now you all want the same thing, which you call the Deep Truth?'

'Yes, O master,' they chorused.

'Have you never heard the saying that there are "as many Ways as there are hearts of men"?' asked the head. 'In any case, here are your ways:

'The First Dervish will travel through the Country of Fools; the Second Dervish will have to find the Magic Mirror; the Third Dervish will have to call in the aid of the Jinn of the Whirlpool.' So saying, he disappeared.

There was some discussion about this, not only because the dervishes wanted more information before setting out, but also because although they had all practised different ways, each yet believed that there was only one way—his own, of course. Now none was certain that his own way was useful enough even though it had been partly responsible for summoning the apparition which they had just seen, and whose very name was unknown to them.

Yak-Baba left the cell first, and instead of asking everyone, as had been his custom, where a learned man might live in the neighbourhood, he asked whoever he met if they knew the Country of Fools. At last, after many months, someone did know, and he set off there. As soon as he entered the Country he saw a woman carrying a door on her back. 'Woman,' he asked, 'why are you doing that?'

'Because this morning before my husband left for his work he said, "Wife, there are valuables in the house. Let nobody pass this door." When I went out I took the door with me, so that nobody could pass it. Now please let *me* pass *you*.'

'Do you want me to tell you something which will make it unnecessary to carry that door about with you?' asked Dervish Yak-Baba. 'Certainly not,' she said. 'The only thing that would help would be if you could tell me how to lighten the actual weight of the door.'

'That I cannot do,' said the Dervish. And so they parted.

A little way further on he met a group of people. They were cowering in terror before a large water-melon which had grown in a field. 'We have never seen one of these monsters before,' they told him, 'and it will certainly grow even larger and will kill us all. But we are afraid to touch it.'

'Would you like me to tell you something about it?' he asked them.

'Don't be a fool!' they replied. 'Kill it and you will be rewarded, but we don't want to know anything about it.' So the dervish took out a knife, advanced upon the melon and cut a slice, which he started to eat.

Amid terrible cries of alarm, the people gave him a handful of money. As he left, they said: 'Please do not come back, Honoured Murderer of Monsters. Do not come and kill us likewise!'

Thus, gradually, he learned that in the Country of the Fools, in order to survive, one must be able to think and talk like a fool as well. After several years he managed to convert some fools to reason, and as a reward one day he attained Deep Knowledge. But although he became a saint in the Country of the Fools, they remembered him only as the Man who Cut Open the Green Monster and Drank its Blood. They tried to do the same, to gain Deep Knowledge—and they never gained it.

Meanwhile, Do-Agha, the Second Dervish, set off on his search for the Deep Knowledge. Instead of asking everywhere he went for the local sages or new exercises and postures, he just asked if anyone had heard of the Magic Mirror. Many misleading answers were given to him, but at last he realized where it might be. It was suspended in a well by a piece of string as fine as a hair, and it was itself only a fragment, because it was made up of the thoughts of men, and there were not enough thoughts to make a whole mirror.

When he had outwitted the demon who guarded it, Do-Agha gazed into the mirror and asked for the Deep Knowledge. Instantly it was his. He settled down and taught in happiness for many years. But because his disciples did not maintain the same degree of concentration needed to renew the mirror regularly, it vanished away. Yet to this day there are people who gaze into mirrors, thinking that this is the Magic Mirror of Do-Agha, the Dervish.

As for the Third Dervish, Se-Kalandar, he looked everywhere for the Jinn of the Whirlpool. This Jinn was known by many other names, but the Kalandar did not know this, and for years he criss-crossed the Jinn's tracks, always missing him because he was not there known as a Jinn or was perhaps not referred to as being connected with a whirlpool.

Finally, after many years, he came to a village and asked: 'O people! has anyone here heard of the Jinn of the Whirlpool?'

'I have never heard of the Jinn,' said someone, 'but this village is called the Whirlpool.'

The Kalandar threw himself upon the ground and cried: 'I will not leave this spot until the Jinn of the Whirlpool appears to me!'

The Jinn, who was lurking near by, swirled up to him and said:

'We do not like strangers near our village, dervish. So I have come to you. What is it you seek?'

'I seek Deep Knowledge, and I have been told under such-and-such-circumstances that you can tell me how to find it.'

'I can indeed,' said the Jinn. 'You have been through much. All that remains for you is to say such-and-such a phrase, sing such-and-such a song, do such-and-such an action; and avoid such-and-such another action. Then you will gain Deep Knowledge.'

The Dervish thanked the Jinn and began his programme. Months passed, then years, until he was performing his devotions and exercises correctly. People came and watched him and then began to copy him, because of his zeal, and because he was known to be a devout and worthy man.

Eventually the Dervish attained to Deep Knowledge; leaving behind him a devoted assembly of people who continued his ways. They never did attain to Deep Knowledge, of course, because they were beginning at the end of the Dervish's course of study.

Afterwards, whenever any of the adherents of these three dervishes meet, one says: 'I have my mirror here. Gaze enough and you will eventually attain Deep Knowledge.'

Another replies: 'Sacrifice a melon, it will help you as it did Dervish Yak-Baba.'

A third interrupts: 'Nonsense! The only way is to persevere in the study and organizing of certain postures, of prayer and good works.'

When they had in fact attained to Deep Knowledge, the Three Dervishes found that they were powerless to help those whom they had left behind: as when a man carried away on a running tide may see a landlubber pursued by a leopard, and be unable to go to his help.

The adventures of these men—their names mean 'one', 'two' and 'three' respectively—are sometimes taken as a satire upon conventional religion.

This is a summary of a famous teaching-story, 'What Befell the Three'. It is attributed to the Sufi teacher, Murad Shami, the chief of the Muradis, who died in 1719. The dervishes who relate this tale claim that it has an interior message far more important in a practical way than the superficial meaning.

The Four Magic Treasures

Four holy dervishes of the second rank met together and determined that they would search the face of the whole earth for objects which would enable them to help mankind. They had studied everything they could, and had realized that by this kind of cooperation they would be able to serve best.

They arranged among themselves to meet again after thirty years.

On the appointed day they came together again. The first brought with him from the farthest North a magical staff. Whoever rode upon it could reach his destination instantly. The second, from the farthest West, had brought a magical hood. Whoever put it over his head could immediately change his appearance to resemble anyone in existence. The third, from his travels and searches in the farthest East, brought a magic mirror. In this any part of the world could be seen at will. The fourth dervish, working in the farthest South, had brought back with him a magical cup, with which any disease could be healed.

Thus equipped, the dervishes looked into the Mirror, to find the source of the Water of Life, which would enable them to live long enough to put these articles to effective use. They found the Fountain of Life, flew to it on the magic staff, and drank of the Water.

Then they performed an invocation, to see who was most in need of their services. Into the Mirror swam the face of a man who was almost on the point of death. He was many days' journey away.

The dervishes at once mounted their magic staff and flew, in the twinkling of an eye, to the house of the sick man.

'We are famous healers,' they said to the man at the gate, 'who understand that your master is ill. Admit us and we will help him.'

When the sick man heard this he ordered the dervishes to be

brought to his bedside. As soon as he saw them, however, he became worse, almost as if seized by a fit. They were ejected from his presence, while one of the attendants explained that the patient was an enemy of dervishes and hated them.

Putting their heads one by one into the magical hood, they changed their appearances so that they were agreeable to the sick man, and presented themselves again, this time as four different healers.

As soon as the man had drunk some medicine from the Magic Cup he was better than he had ever been in his life. He was delighted—and, being rich, rewarded the dervishes with a house of his own into which they settled.

They continued to live in this house, and every day they went their separate ways, using the magical apparatus which they had brought together, for the good of mankind.

One day, however, when the other dervishes were out on their rounds, soldiers arrived and arrested the dervish with the healing Cup. The king of that country had heard about this great doctor, and had sent for him to cure his daughter, who was suffering from a strange illness.

The dervish was taken to the princess's bedside, and he offered her some medicine of her own, but in the special Cup. But, because he had been unable to consult the magic Mirror for the cure, it did not work.

The princess was no better, and the king ordered the dervish to be nailed up on a wall. He begged for some time to consult his friends, but the king was impatient and believed that this was just a stratagem, and that the dervish might escape.

As soon as the other dervishes got home, they looked in the magic Mirror to find where their companion had gone. Seeing him on the point of death, they sped on the magic Staff to his aid. They saved him in the nick of time. But they were unable to save the king's daughter, because the cup was nowhere to be found.

Looking in the magic Mirror, the dervishes saw that it had been thrown, by the king's order, into the depths of the deepest ocean in the world.

In spite of the miraculous apparatus at their disposal, it took them a thousand years to recover the cup. Ever after the experience with the princess, these four dervishes made it their practice to work in secret, making it appear, through skilful arrangement, that whatever they did for the good of mankind would appear to have been done in some easily explicable way.

୨୭

This legend resembles many Eastern stories about magical apparatus, often found in folklore recitals.

Some see in it a disguised reference to the claim that Jesus did not die on the Cross. Others hold that it refers to the four techniques of the major Eastern Dervish schools and their amalgamation under the Naqshbandis in India and Khorasan.

The more usual Sufi explanation is that the 'dervish work' consists of four elements which must be applied together and in secrecy.

The Dreams and the Loaf of Bread

THREE travellers on a long and exhausting journey had become companions, and shared the same pleasures and sorrows, pooling all their resources.

After many days they realized that all they had between them was a piece of bread and a mouthful of water in a flask. They fell to quarrelling as to who should have all the food. Making no progress on this score, they tried to divide the bread and water. Still they could not arrive at a conclusion.

As dusk was falling, one finally suggested that they should sleep. When they awoke, the person who had had the most remarkable dream would decide what should be done.

The next morning the three rose as the sun came up.

'This is my dream,' said the first: 'I was carried away to places such as cannot be described, so wonderful and serene were they. I met a wise man who said to me: "You deserve the food, for your past and future life are worthy and suitable subjects for admiration."'

'How strange,' said the second man. 'For in my dream, I actually saw all my past and my future. In my future I saw a man of all-knowledge, who said: "You deserve the bread more than your friends, for you are more learned and patient. You must be well-nurtured, for you are destined to lead men."'

The third traveller said: 'In my dream I saw nothing, heard nothing, said nothing. I felt a compelling presence which forced me to get up, find the bread and water—and consume them then and there. And this is what I did.'

ꙮ

The Dreams and the Loaf of Bread

This tale is one of a number attributed to Shah Mohammed Gwath Shattari, who died in 1563. He wrote the famous treatise, *Five Jewels*, in which the manner of man's attainment of higher states is described in the terminology of magic and sorcery, based on ancient models. He was an initiating Master of no less than fourteen Orders and greatly esteemed by the Indian Emperor Humayun.

Although hailed by some as a saint, some of his writings were considered by clerics to infringe holy writ, and they therefore sought his execution. He was ultimately acquitted of heresy on the grounds that things said in a special state of mind could not be judged by ordinary scholastic standards. His shrine is at Gwalior: a very important Sufi place of pilgrimage.

The same plot is used in monkish Christian tales of the Middle Ages.

Bread and Jewels

A KING once decided to give away a part of his wealth by disinterested charity. At the same time he wanted to watch what happened to it. So he called a baker whom he could trust and told him to bake two loaves of bread. In the first was to be baked a number of jewels, and in the other, nothing but flour and water.

These were to be given to the most and least pious people whom the baker could find.

The following morning two men presented themselves at the oven. One was dressed as a dervish and seemed most pious, though he was in reality a mere pretender. The other, who said nothing at all, reminded the baker of a man whom he did not like, by a coincidence of facial resemblance.

The baker gave the bread with the jewels in it to the man in the dervish robe, and the ordinary loaf to the second man.

As soon as he got his loaf the false dervish felt it and weighed it in his hand. He felt the jewels, and to him they seemed like lumps in the loaf, unblended flour. He weighed the bread in his hand, and the weight of the jewels made it seem to him to be too heavy. He looked at the baker, and realized that he was not a man to trifle with. So he turned to the second man and said: 'Why not exchange your loaf for mine? You look hungry, and this one is larger.'

The second man, prepared to accept whatever befell, willingly exchanged loaves.

The king, who was watching through a crack in the bakehouse door, was surprised, but did not realize the relative merits of the two men.

The false dervish got the ordinary loaf. The king concluded that Fate had intervened to keep the dervish protected from wealth. The really good man found the jewels and was able to make good use of them. The king could not interpret this happening.

'I did what I was told to do,' said the baker.

'You cannot tamper with Fate,' said the king.

'How clever I was!' said the false dervish.

∾

This tale is recited at Gazargah, the shrine in Western Afghanistan where the great Sufi teacher Khakja Abdullah Ansar was buried in 1089. Its 'first layer' of teaching is that while man may be offered something of great value to his future, he does not necessarily take advantage of it.

The Limitations of Dogma

ONE day the great Sultan Mahmud was in the streets of Ghazna, his capital. He saw a poor porter struggling under the weight of a heavy stone which he was carrying on his back. Moved by pity for his condition and unable to restrain his compassion, Mahmud called out to him, in royal command:

'Drop that stone, porter.'

Immediately he was obeyed. The stone lay there, an obstacle to all who tried to pass, for years on end. Ultimately a number of citizens interceded with the king, asking him to give a command for the stone to be taken away.

But Mahmud, reflecting in administrative wisdom, felt himself bound to reply:

'That which has been done by command cannot be rescinded by an equal command, lest the people think that imperial orders are motivated by whims. Let the stone remain where it is.'

The stone remained, therefore, for the rest of Mahmud's lifetime. Even when he was dead, from respect for royal commands, it was not moved.

The story was well known. People took its meaning in one of three ways, each according to his capacity. Those who were against rulership considered that it was an evidence of the stupidity of authority trying to maintain itself. Those who revered power felt respect for commands, however inconvenient. Those who understood aright penetrated the moral intended by the king, regardless of his reputation among the unheedy. For, by causing to be placed in that inconvenient position an obstacle, and giving currency to his reasons for leaving it there, Mahmud was telling those who could understand to obey temporal authority, but to realize that those who rule by inflexible dogma cannot be of complete use to humankind.

Those who read the lesson therefore swelled the ranks of the truth-seekers, and many thus found their way to Truth.

❧

This story, without the subtlety of interpretation which appears here, is found in the celebrated classic, *Akhlaq-i-Mohsini*, ('Beneficent Ethics') of Hasan Waiz Kashifi.

The present version forms part of the teaching of the Sufi sheikh Daud of Qandahar, who died in 1965. It provides an ideal expression of the various levels of understanding of actions by people who judge in accordance with their training. The indirect method of illustration used by Sultan Mahmud is classically a Sufic one, summed up in the phrase: 'Speak to the wall, so that the door may hear.'

The Fisherman and the Genie

A LONE fisherman one day brought up a brass bottle, stoppered with lead, in his net. Though the appearance of the bottle was quite different from what he was used to finding in the sea, he thought it might contain something of value. Besides, he had not had a good catch, and at the worst he could sell the bottle to a brass-merchant.

The bottle was not very large. On the top was inscribed a strange symbol, the Seal of Solomon, King and Master. Inside had been imprisoned a fearsome genie; and the bottle had been cast into the sea by Solomon himself so that men should be protected from the spirit until such time as there came one who could control it, assigning it to its proper role of service of mankind.

But the fishermen knew nothing of this. All he knew was that here was something which he could investigate, which might be of profit to him. Its outside shone and it was a work of art. 'Inside,' he thought, 'there may be diamonds.'

Forgetting the adage, 'Man can use only what he has learned to use,' the fisherman pulled out the leaden stopper.

He inverted the bottle, but there seemed to be nothing in it, so he set it down and looked at it. Then he noticed a faint wisp as of smoke, slowly becoming denser, which swirled and formed itself into the appearance of a huge and threatening being, which addressed him in a booming voice:

'I am the Chief of the Jinns who know the secrets of miraculous happenings, imprisoned by order of Solomon against whom I rebelled, and I shall destroy you!'

The fisherman was terrified, and, casting himself upon the sand, cried out: 'Will you destroy him who gave you your freedom?'

'Indeed I shall,' said the genie, 'for rebellion is my nature, and destruction is my capacity, although I may have been rendered immobile for several thousand years.'

The fisherman now saw that, far from profit from this unwelcome catch, he was likely to be annihilated for no good reason that he could fathom.

He looked at the seal upon the stopper, and suddenly an idea occurred to him. 'You could never have come out of that bottle,' he said. 'It is too small.'

'What! Do you doubt the word of the Master of the Jinns?' roared the apparition. And he dissolved himself again into wispy smoke and went back into the bottle. The fisherman took up the stopper and plugged the bottle with it.

Then he threw it back, as far as he could, into the depths of the sea.

Many years passed, until one day another fisherman, grandson of the first, cast his net in the same place, and brought up the self-same bottle.

He placed the bottle upon the sand and was about to open it when a thought struck him. It was the piece of advice which had been passed down to him by his father, from *his* father.

It was: 'Man can use only what he has learned to use.'

And so it was that when the genie, aroused from his slumbers by the movement of his metal prison, called through the brass: 'Son of Adam, whoever you may be, open the stopper of this bottle and release me: for I am the Chief of the Jinns who know the secrets of miraculous happenings,' the young fisherman, remembering his ancestral adage, placed the bottle carefully in a cave and scaled the heights of a near-by cliff, seeking the cell of a wise man who lived there.

He told the story to the wise man, who said: 'Your adage is perfectly true: and you have to do this thing yourself, though you must know how to do it.'

'But what do I have to do?' asked the youth.

'There is something, surely, that you feel you want to do?' said the other.

'What I want to do is to release the jinn, so that he can give me miraculous knowledge: or perhaps mountains of gold, and seas made from emeralds, and all the other things which jinns can bestow.'

'It has not, of course, occurred to you', said the sage, 'that the jinn might not give you these things when released; or that he may give them to you and then take them away because you have no means to guard them; quite apart from what might befall you if and when you did have such things, since "Man can use only what he has learned to use." '

'Then what should I do?'

'Seek from the jinn a sample of what he can offer. Seek a means of safeguarding that sample and testing it. Seek knowledge, not possessions, for possessions without knowledge are useless, and that is the cause of all our distractions.'

Now, because he was alert and reflective, the young man worked out his plan on the way back to the cave where he had left the jinn.

He tapped on the bottle, and the jinn's voice answered, tinny through the metal, but still terrible: 'In the name of Solomon the Mighty, upon whom be peace, release me, son of Adam!'

'I don't believe that you are who you say and that you have the powers which you claim,' answered the youth.

'Don't believe me! Do you not know that I am incapable of telling a lie?' the jinn roared back.

'No, I do not,' said the fisherman.

'Then how can I convince you?'

'By giving me a demonstration. Can you exercise any powers through the wall of the bottle?'

'Yes,' admitted the jinn, 'but I cannot release myself through these powers.'

'Very well, then, give me the ability to know the truth of the problem which is on my mind.'

Instantly, as the jinn exercised his strange craft, the fisherman became aware of the source of the adage handed down by his grandfather. He saw, too, the whole scene of the release of the jinn from the bottle; and he also saw how he could convey to others how to gain such capacities from the jinns. But he also realized that there was no more that he could do. And so the fisherman picked up the bottle and, like his grandfather, cast it into the ocean.

And he spent the rest of his life not as a fisherman but as a man who tried to explain to others the perils of 'Man trying to use what he has not learned to use.'

But, since few people ever came across jinns in bottles, and there was no wise man to prompt them in any case, the successors of the fisherman garbled what they called his 'teachings', and mimed his descriptions. In due course they became a religion, with brazen bottles from which they sometimes drank housed in costly and well-adorned temples. And, because they respected the behaviour of this fisherman, they strove to emulate his actions and his deportment in every way.

The bottle, now many centuries later, remains the holy symbol and mystery for these people. They try to love each other only because they love this fisherman; and in the place where he settled and built a humble shack they deck themselves with finery and move in elaborate rituals.

Unknown to them the disciples of the wise man still live, the descendants of the fisherman are unknown. The brass bottle lies at the bottom of the sea with the genie slumbering within.

ॐ

This story, in one version, is well known to readers of the *Arabian Nights*. The form in which it is given here represents its use by dervishes. It is noteworthy that 'knowledge gained from a genie' in a similar manner is said to have been the source of the power of both Virgil the Enchanter of the Middle Ages, in Naples; and also of Gerbert, who became Pope Sylvester II in A.D. 999.

The Time, the Place and the People

෨෬෨෬෨෬෨෬෨෬෨෬෨෬෨෬෨෬෨෬෨෬෨෬෨෬෨෬෨෬෨෬෨෬෨෬

IN ANCIENT times there was a king who called a dervish to him and said:

'The dervish Path, through a succession of masters reaching back in unbroken succession to the earliest days of man, has always provided the light which has been the motivating cause of the very values of which my kingship is no more than a wan reflection.'

The dervish answered: 'It is so.'

'Now,' said the king, 'since I am so enlightened as to know the foregoing facts, eager and willing to learn the truths which you, in your superior wisdom, can make available — teach me!'

'Is that a command or a request?' asked the dervish.

'It is whatever you make of it,' said the king, 'for if it will work as a command, I shall learn. If it operates successfully as a request, I shall learn.'

And he waited for the dervish to speak.

Many minutes passed, and at length the dervish lifted his head from the attitude of contemplation and said:

'You must await the "moment of transmission".'

This confused the king, for, after all, if he wanted to learn he felt he had a right to be told, or shown, something or other.

The dervish left the court.

After that, day after day, the dervish continued to attend upon the king. Day in and day out the affairs of state were transacted, the kingdom passed through times of joy and trial, the counsellors of state gave their advice, the wheel of heaven revolved.

'The dervish comes here every day,' thought the king, each time he caught sight of the figure in the patched cloak, 'and yet he never refers to our conversation about learning. True, he takes part in many of the activities of the Court; he talks and he laughs, he eats and he, no doubt, sleeps. Is he waiting for a sign of some kind?' But, try as he might, the king was unable to plumb the depths of this mystery.

At length, when the appropriate wave of the unseen lapped upon the shore of possibility, a conversation was taking place at court. Someone was saying: 'Daud of Sahil is the greatest singer in the world.'

And the king, although ordinarily this sort of statement did not move him, conceived a powerful desire to hear this singer.

'Have him brought before me,' he commanded.

The master of ceremonies was sent to the singer's house, but Daud, monarch among singers, merely replied: 'This king of yours knows little of the requirements of singing. If he wants me just to look at my face, I will come. But if he wants to hear me sing, he will have to wait, like everyone else, until I am in the right mood to do so. It is knowing when to perform and when not which has made me, as it would make any ass which knew the secret, into a great singer.'

When this message was taken to the king, he alternated between wrath and desire, and called out: 'Is there nobody here who will force this man to sing for me? For, if he sings only when the mood takes him, I, for my part, want to hear him while I still want to hear him.'

It was then that the dervish stepped forward and said:

'Peacock of the age, come with me to visit this singer.'

The courtiers nudged one another. Some thought that the dervish had been playing a deep game, and was now gambling upon making the singer perform. If he succeeded, the king would surely reward him. But they remained silent, for they feared a possible challenge.

Without a word the king stood up and commanded a poor garment to be brought. Putting it on, he followed the dervish into the street.

The disguised king and his guide soon found themselves at the singer's house. When they knocked, Daud called down:

'I am not singing today, so go away and leave me in peace.'

At this the dervish, seating himself upon the ground, began to sing. He sang Daud's favourite piece, and he sang it right through, from beginning to end.

The king, who was no great connoisseur, was very much moved by the song, and his attention was diverted to the sweetness of the dervish's voice. He did not know that the dervish had sung the song slightly off-key deliberately, in order to awaken a desire to correct it in the heart of the master-singer.

'Please, please, do sing it again,' begged the king, 'for I have never heard such a sweet melody.'

But at that moment Daud himself began to sing. At the very first notes the dervish and the king were as men transfixed, and their attention was riveted to the notes as they flowed faultlessly from the throat of the nightingale of Sahil.

When the song was finished, the king sent a lavish present to Daud. To the dervish he said: 'Man of Wisdom! I admire your skill in provoking the Nightingale to perform, and I would like to make you an adviser at the court.'

But the dervish simply said: 'Majesty, you can hear the song you wish only if there is a singer, if you are present, and if there is someone to form the channel for the performance of the song. As it is with master-singers and kings, so it is with dervishes and their students. The time, the place, the people and the skills.'

∞

The clash between the Sufis and the ordinary scholastic is strongly manifested in the theory that Sufi ideas can only be studied in accordance with certain principles: and these include time, place and people.

Scholars demand verification of Sufi claims on their own terms. Many Sufi stories illustrate, like this one, that Sufis only claim an equal chance of arranging conditions to those required by academics or scientists.

This tale is from the teaching of Sayed Imam Ali Shah, who died in 1860 and whose shrine is at Gurdaspur, in India.

This famous Naqshbandi teacher was frequently plagued by would-be disciples of all origins and faiths because of the strange 'psi' phenomena constantly reported of him. People said that he appeared to them in dreams, giving them important information; that he was seen in several places at once; that whatever he said was found to have some application to the advantage of his interlocutor. But when they came face to face with him, people could find nothing supernatural or unusual about him.

The Parable of the Three Domains

HUMAN life, and the life of communities, is not what it seems. In fact, it follows a pattern evident to some and concealed to others. Again, more than one pattern is moving at a time. Yet men take one part of one pattern and try to weld it with another. They invariably find what they expect, not what is really there.

Let us consider, for example, three things: the wheat in the field, the water in the stream, and the salt in the mine. This is the condition of natural man; he is a being which is both complete in some senses and has further uses and capacities in further senses.

Each of the three items is representative here of substances in a state of potentiality. They may remain as they are, or circumstances (and in the case of man, effort) may transform them.

This is the condition of the First Domain, or state of man.

In the Second Domain, however, we have a stage in which something further can be done. The wheat, by effort and knowledge, is collected and ground into flour. The water is taken from the stream and stored for a further use. The salt is extracted and refined. This is a Domain of a different activity than the first, which was merely growing. In this Domain, stored knowledge is brought into play.

The Third Domain can come into being only after the three ingredients, in correct quantity and proportion, have been assembled in a certain place, at a certain time. The salt, water and flour are mixed and kneaded to become dough. When the yeast is brought, a living element is added; and the oven is made ready for the baking of the loaf. This making depends as much upon 'touch' as upon stored knowledge.

Everything will behave in accordance with its situation: and its situation is the Domain in which it is cast.

If the objective is bread, why talk of salt-making?

ოჯ

This story, originating with the Sarmoun Sufis, echoes the teaching of Ghazali that 'the ignorant man has no real idea of the learning of the scholastic. Equally, the scholastic has no adequate conception of the knowledge of the Enlightened Man.'

It also underlines the dervish belief that traditionalist religious, metaphysical or philosophical schools are continuing to 'grind flour' and cannot progress further, lacking the presence of men of insight, who appear only rarely.

Valuable — and Worthless

A CERTAIN king one day called a counsellor to him and said: 'The strength of real thinking depends upon the examination of alternatives. Tell me which alternative is better: to increase the knowledge of my people or to give them more to eat. In either case they will benefit.'

The Sufi said: 'Majesty, there is no point in giving knowledge to those who cannot receive it, any more than there is point in giving food to those who cannot understand your motives. Therefore it is not correct to assume that "in either case they will benefit". If they cannot digest the food, or if they think you give it to them as a bribe, or that they can get more — you have failed. If they cannot see that they are being given knowledge, or whether it is knowledge or not, or even why you are giving it to them — they will not benefit. Therefore the question must be taken by degrees. The first degree is the consideration: "The most valuable person is worthless and the most worthless person is valuable."'

'Demonstrate this truth to me, for I cannot understand it,' said the king.

The Sufi then called the chief dervish of Afghanistan, and he came to the Court. 'If you had your way, what would you have someone in Kabul do?' he asked.

'It so happens that there is a man near such-and-such a place who, if he knew it, could by giving a pound of cherries to a certain necessitous man, gain a fortune for himself and also great advancement for the whole country and progress for the Path,' said the chief dervish, who knew of the inner correspondence of things.

The king was excited, for Sufis do not generally discourse upon such things. 'Call him here and we will have it done!' he cried. The others silenced him with a gesture. 'No,' said the first Sufi, 'this cannot work unless it is done voluntarily.'

In disguise, in order not to influence the man's choice, the three of them went straight to the Kabul bazaar. Divested of his turban and robe, the chief Sufi looked very much like any ordinary man. 'I will take the part of the exciting cause,' he whispered, as the group stood looking at the fruit. He approached the greengrocer and wished him good day. Then he said: 'I know a poor man. Will you give him a pound of cherries, as a charity?' The greengrocer bellowed with laughter. 'Well, I have heard some tricks, but this is the first time that someone who wanted cherries has stooped to ask me as if it were for charity!'

'You see what I mean?' the first Sufi asked the king. 'The most valuable man we have has just made the most valuable suggestion, and the event has proved that he is worthless to the man to whom he speaks.'

'But what about "the most worthless person" being valuable?' asked the king.

The two dervishes beckoned him to follow them.

As they were about to cross the Kabul River, the two Sufis suddenly seized the king and threw him into the water. He could not swim.

As he felt himself about to drown, Kaka Divana—whose name means Insane Uncle—a well-known pauper and lunatic who roamed the streets, jumped in and brought him safely to the bank. Various other, more solid, citizens had seen him in the water, but none moved.

When the king was somewhat restored, the two dervishes intoned together: 'The most worthless person is valuable!'

So the king went back to his old, traditional method of giving whatever he could—whether education or help of any kind—to those whom it was decided from time to time were the most worthy recipients of such aid.

ಞ

Sufi Abdul-Hamid Khan of Qandahar, who died in 1962, was Master of the Afghan Mint, and a dervish Ancient who had mastered Western technology. Among the many teaching-stories attributed to him is this one.

The king involved is said to have been the late Nadir Shah of Afghanistan, whom the Sufi served, and who died in 1933. The succession of events, however, is based on an earlier story: but this king may not have heard it before.

The Bird and the Egg

ONCE upon a time there was a bird which did not have the power of flight. Like a chicken, he walked about on the ground, although he knew that some birds did fly.

It so happened that, through a combination of circumstances, the egg of a flying bird was incubated by this flightless one.

In due time the chick came forth, still with the potentiality for flight which he had always had, even from the time when he was in the egg.

It spoke to its foster-parent, saying: 'When will I fly?' And the landbound bird said: 'Persist in your attempts to fly, just like the others.'

For he did not know how to take the fledgeling for its lesson in flying: even how to topple it from the nest so that it might learn.

And it is curious, in a way, that the young bird did not see this. His recognition of the situation was confused by the fact that he felt gratitude to the bird which had hatched him.

'Without this service', he said to himself, 'surely I would still be in the egg?'

And, again, sometimes he said to himself: 'Anyone who can hatch me, surely he can teach me to fly. It must be just a matter of time, or of my own unaided efforts, or of some great wisdom: yes, that is it. Suddenly one day I will be carried to the next stage by him who has brought me thus far.'

ⁿ

This tale appears in various forms in different versions of Suhrawardi's twelfth-century *Awarif el-Maarif* and carries many messages. It is said to be capable of interpretation intuitively in accordance with the level of consciousness reached by the student. On the obvious level it has, of course, morals, some of them emphasizing the very bases of modern civilization. These include:

'To assume that one thing follows from another can be absurd and prevent further progress,' and 'Just because some-one can perform one function does not prove that he can fulfil another.'

Three Pieces of Advice

A MAN once caught a bird. The bird said to him, 'I am no use to you as a captive. But let me free, and I will tell you three valuable pieces of advice.'

The bird promised to give the first piece of advice while still in the man's grasp, the second when he reached a branch, the third after he had gained the top of a mountain.

The man agreed, and asked for the first piece of advice.

The bird said:

'If you lose something, even if it be valued by you as much as life itself—do not regret it.'

Now the man let the bird go, and it hopped to a branch.

It continued with the second piece of advice:

'Never believe anything which is contrary to sense, without proof.'

Then the bird flew to the mountain-top. From here it said:

'O unfortunate one! Within me are two huge jewels, and if you had only killed me they would have been yours!'

The man was anguished at the thought of what he had lost, but he said: 'At least now tell me the third piece of advice.'

The bird replied:

'What a fool you are, asking for more advice when you have not given thought to the first two pieces! I told you not to worry about what had been lost, and not to believe in something contrary to sense. Now you are doing both. You are believing something ridiculous and grieving because you have lost something! I am not big enough to have inside me huge jewels.

'You are a fool. Therefore you must stay within the usual restrictions imposed on man.'

In dervish circles, this tale is regarded as of very great importance in 'sensitizing' the mind of the student, preparing it for experiences which cannot be elicited in ordinary ways.

In addition to being in daily use among Sufis, the story is found in the Rumi classic, the *Mathnavi*. It is featured in the *Divine Book* of Attar, one of the teachers of Rumi. Both men lived in the thirteenth century.

The Mountain Path

AN INTELLIGENT man, a scholar with a trained mind, came one day to a village. He wanted to compare, as an exercise and a study, the different points of view which might be represented there.

He went to the caravanserai and asked for the most truthful inhabitant and also the greatest liar of the village. The people who were there agreed unanimously that the man called Kazzab was their greatest liar; and that Rastgu was the truthful one. In turn he visited them, asking each a simple question: 'What is the best way to the next village?'

Rastgu the Truthful said: 'The mountain path.'

Kazzab the Liar also said: 'The mountain path.'

Not unnaturally, this puzzled the traveller a great deal.

So he asked a few others, ordinary citizens.

Some said: 'The river;' others: 'Across the fields.'

And others again said: 'The mountain path.'

He took the mountain path, but in addition to the matter of the goal of his journey, the problem of the truthful and the liars of the village troubled him.

When he got to the next village, and related his story at the resthouse, he ended: 'I evidently made the basic logical mistake of asking the wrong people for the names of the Truthful and the Liar. I arrived here quite easily, by the mountain path.'

A wise man who was present spoke. 'Logicians, it must be admitted, tend to be blind, and have to ask others to help them. But the matter here is otherwise. The facts are thus: The river is the easiest route, so the liar suggested the mountain. But the truthful man was not only truthful. He noticed that you had a donkey, which made the journey easy enough. The liar happened to be unobservant of the fact that you had no boat: otherwise he would have suggested the river.'

'People find the capacities and blessings of the Sufis impossible to believe. But such people are those who have no knowledge of real belief. They believe all kinds of things which are not true, because of habit or because they are told them by people of authority.

'Real belief is something else. Those who are capable of real belief are those who have experienced a thing. When they have experienced ... capacities and blessings merely reported are of no use to them.' These words, reported of Sayed Shah (Qadiri, who died in 1854) sometimes precede 'The Mountain Path'.

The Snake and the Peacock

One day a youth named Adi, The Calculator—because he had studied mathematics—decided to leave Bokhara and seek greater knowledge. His teacher advised him to travel southwards, and said: 'Seek the meaning of the Peacock and the Snake:' something which gave young Adi a great deal to think about.

He travelled through Khorasan and finally to Iraq. In the latter place he actually came across a place where there was a peacock and a snake, and Adi spoke to them. 'We are having a discussion', they said, 'about our relative merits.'

'This is just what I want to study,' said Adi, 'so pray speak on.'

'I feel that I am the more important,' said the Peacock. 'I represent aspiration, flight into the heavens, the celestial beauty, and hence knowledge of the higher things. It is my mission to remind man, by mime, of aspects of his self which are hidden to him.'

'I, on the other hand,' said the Snake, hissing slightly, 'represent just the same things. Like man, I am bound to the earth. This makes me remind him of himself. Like him, I am flexible, as I wind my way along the ground. He often forgets this, too. In tradition, I am he who stands guard over treasures, hidden in the earth.'

'But you are loathsome!' shouted the Peacock. 'You are sly, secretive, dangerous.'

'You list my human characteristics,' said the Snake, 'while I prefer to list my other functions, as I have already done. Now look at you:

'You are vain, over-plump, and have a harsh cry. Your feet are too big, your feathers too well-developed.'

Adi interrupted at this point. 'It is only your disagreement which has enabled me to see that neither of you is altogether right. And yet we can clearly see, if we take away your personal preoccupations, that *together* you make up a message for mankind.'

And Adi, while the two opponents listened, was able to explain to them what their functions were.

'Man crawls on the ground like the Snake. He could rise to the heights like a bird. But, just as the Snake is covetous, he retains this selfishness when he tries to rise, and becomes like the peacock, over-proud. In the peacock we can see possibility of man, but not properly achieved. In the sheen on the Snake we can see the possibility of beauty. In the Peacock we see it taking a flamboyant turn.'

And then a Voice from within spoke to Adi and told him: 'That is not all. These two creatures are both endowed with life: that is their determining factor. They fight because each has settled for his own kind of life, thinking it to be the realization of a true status. One, however, guards treasure and cannot use it. The other reflects beauty, a treasure, but cannot transform himself with it. In spite of their not having taken advantage of what was open to them, they yet symbolize it, for those who can see and hear.'

জ

Considered a mystery by Orientalists, the Cult of the Snake and Peacock in Iraq was founded on the teaching of a Sufi Sheikh, Adi, son of Musafir, in the twelfth century.

This story, preserved in legend, shows how the dervish masters shaped their 'schools' around various symbols, chosen to illustrate their doctrine.

In Arabic, 'Peacock' also stands for 'adornment'; while 'Snake' has the same letter-form as 'organism' and 'life'. Hence the symbolism of the cryptic Peacock Angel Cult — the Yezidis — is a way of indicating 'The Interior and the External', traditional Sufi formulae.

The Cult still exists in the Middle East, and has adherents (none of them known to be Iraqis) in Britain and the United States.

The Water of Paradise

HARITH the Bedouin and his wife Nafisa, moving from place to place, pitched their ragged tent wherever a few date palms, grazing scrub for their camel or a pool of brackish water were to be found. This had been their way of life for many years, and Harith seldom varied his daily round: trapping desert rats for their skins, twisting ropes from palm fibres to sell to passing caravans.

One day, however, a new spring appeared in the sands, and Harith scooped a little of the water into his mouth. To him this seemed the very water of paradise, for it was far less foul than his usual drink. To us it would have seemed repulsively full of salt. 'This', he said, 'I must take to one who will appreciate it.'

He accordingly set off for Baghdad and the palace of Haroun el-Raschid, travelling without pausing to do more than munch a few dates. Harith took two goatskins of water: one for himself, the other for the Caliph.

Days later he reached Baghdad, and marched straight to the palace. The guards listened to his tale and, only because it was the rule, they admitted him to the public audience of Haroun.

'Commander of the Faithful,' said Harith, 'I am a poor Bedouin, and know all the waters of the desert, though I may know little of other things. I have just discovered this Water of Paradise, and realizing that it was a fitting gift for you, have come at once to make it as an offering.'

Haroun the Straightforward tasted the water and, because he understood his people, he told the guards to take Harith away and lock him up for a time until his decision might be known. Then, calling the captain of the guard, he told him: 'What to us is nothing, to him is everything. Take him, therefore, by night from the palace. Do not let him see the mighty River Tigris. Escort him all the way to his tent without allowing him to taste sweet water.

Then give him a thousand pieces of gold and my thanks for his service. Tell him that he is the guardian of the Water of Paradise, and that he administers it for any traveller in my name, to be freely given away.'

ϗϗ

This is also known as 'The Story of the Two Worlds'. It is related on the authority of Abu el-Atahiyya of the Aniza tribe (a contemporary of Haroun el-Raschid and founder of the *Maskhara* ('Reveller') Dervishes, whose name is perpetuated by Mascara in Western languages. His followers have been traced to Spain, France and other countries.

El-Atahiyya has been called 'the father of Arabic sacred poetry'. He died in 828.

The Horseman and the Snake

⋈⋈⋈⋈⋈⋈⋈⋈⋈⋈⋈⋈⋈⋈⋈⋈⋈⋈⋈⋈⋈⋈⋈⋈⋈⋈⋈⋈⋈

THERE is a proverb that 'the "opposition" of the man of knowledge is better than the "support" of the fool.'

I, Salim Abdali, bear witness that this is true in the greater ranges of existence, as it is true in the lower levels.

This is made manifest in the tradition of the Wise, who have handed down the tale of the Horseman and the Snake.

A horseman from his point of vantage saw a poisonous snake slip down the throat of a sleeping man. The horseman realized that if the man were allowed to sleep the venom would surely kill him.

Accordingly he lashed the sleeper until he was awake. Having no time to lose, he forced this man to a place where there were a number of rotten apples lying upon the ground and made him eat them. Then he made him drink large gulps of water from a stream.

All the while the other man was trying to get away, crying: 'What have I done, you enemy of humanity, that you should abuse me in this manner?'

Finally, when he was near to exhaustion, and dusk was falling, the man fell to the ground and vomited out the apples, the water, and the snake. When he saw what had come out of him, he realized what had happened, and begged the forgiveness of the horseman.

This is our condition. In reading this, do not take history for allegory, nor allegory for history. Those who are endowed with knowledge have responsibility. Those who are not, have none beyond what they can conjecture.

The man who was saved said: 'If you had told me, I would have accepted your treatment with a good grace.'

The horseman answered: 'If I had told you, you would not have believed. Or you would have been paralysed by fright. Or run away. Or gone to sleep again, seeking forgetfulness. And there would not have been time.'

Spurring his horse, the mysterious rider rode away.

∞

Salim Abdali (1700–1765) brought down upon the Sufis almost unprecedented calumnies from intellectuals for claiming that a Sufi master will know what is wrong with a man, and may have to act quickly and paradoxically to save him, thus incurring the fury of those who do not know what he is about.

This story Abdali quotes from Rumi. Even today, there are probably not many people who will concede the claims inherent in the tale. Yet this statement has been accepted in one form or another by all Sufis. Commenting upon this, the master Haidar Gul says only: 'There is a limit beyond which it is unhealthy for mankind to conceal truth in order not to offend those whose minds are closed.'

Isa and the Doubters

IT IS related by the Master Jalaludin Rumi and others that one day Isa, the son of Miryam, was walking in the desert near Jerusalem with a number of people, in whom covetousness was still strong.

They begged Isa to tell them the Secret Name by which Isa restored the dead to life. He said: 'If I tell you, you will abuse it.'

They said: 'We are ready and fitted for such knowledge; besides, it will reinforce our faith.'

'You do not know what you ask,' he said, but he told them the Word.

Soon afterwards, these people were walking in a deserted place when they saw a heap of whitened bones. 'Let us make a trial of the Word,' they said to one another, and they did.

No sooner had the Word been pronounced than the bones became clothed with flesh and retransformed into a ravening wild beast, which tore them to shreds.

Those endowed with reason will understand. Those with little reason can earn it through the study of this account.

&

The Isa of the story is Jesus, the son of Mary. It embodies a similar idea to that of the *Sorcerer's Apprentice*, and it also appears in Rumi's work and again and again in oral dervish legends of Jesus, of which there are a large number.

Tradition invokes as one of its famous 'repeaters' one of the first men ever to carry the title of Sufi: Jabir son of el-Hayyan, the Latin Geber, who is also the founder of Christian alchemy.

He died in about 790. He was originally a Sabean and, according to Western authors, made important chemical discoveries.

In the Street of the Perfume-Sellers

A SCAVENGER, walking down the street of the perfume-sellers, fell down as if dead. People tried to revive him with sweet odours, but he only became worse.

Finally a former scavenger came along, and recognized the situation. He held something filthy under the man's nose and he immediately revived, calling out: 'This is indeed perfume!'

You must prepare yourself for the transition in which there will be none of the things to which you have accustomed yourself. After death your identity will have to respond to stimuli of which you have a chance to get a foretaste here.

If you remain attached to the few things with which you are familiar, it will only make you miserable, as the perfume did the scavenger in the street of the perfume-makers.

ༀ

This parable explains itself. Ghazali uses it in the eleventh-century *Alchemy of Happiness* to underline the Sufi teaching that only some of the things of familiar existence have affinities with the 'other dimension'.

The Parable of the Greedy Sons

THERE was once a hard-working and generous farmer who had several idle and greedy sons. On his deathbed he told them that they would find his treasure if they were to dig in a certain field. As soon as the old man was dead, the sons hurried to the fields, which they dug up from one end to another, and with increasing desperation and concentration when they did not find the gold in the place indicated.

But they found no gold at all. Realizing that in his generosity their father must have given his gold away during his lifetime, they abandoned the search. Finally, it occurred to them that, since the land had been prepared, they might as well now sow a crop They planted wheat, which produced an abundant yield. They sold this crop and prospered that year.

After the harvest was in, the sons thought again about the bare possibility that they might have missed the buried gold, so they again dug up their fields, with the same result.

After several years they became accustomed to labour, and to the cycle of the seasons, something which they had not understood before. Now they understood the reason for their father's method of training them, and they became honest and contented farmers. Ultimately they found themselves possessed of sufficient wealth no longer to wonder about the hidden hoard.

Thus it is with the teaching of the understanding of human destiny and the meaning of life. The teacher, faced with impatience, confusion and covetousness on the part of the students, must direct them to an activity which is known by him to be constructive and beneficial to them, but whose true function and aim is often hidden from them by their own rawness.

THE PARABLE OF THE GREEDY SONS

This story, underlining the claim that a person may develop certain faculties in spite of his attempts to develop others, is unusually widely known. This may be because it carries the preface, 'Those who repeat it will gain more than they know.'

It was published both by the Franciscan, Roger Bacon (who quotes the Sufi philosophy and taught at Oxford, from which he was expelled by order of the Pope) and the seventeenth-century chemist Boerhaave.

This version is attributed to the Sufi, Hasan of Basra, who lived nearly twelve hundred years ago.

The Nature of Discipleship

It is related by Ibrahim Khawwas that when he was a youth he wanted to attach himself to a certain teaching master. He sought out this sage, and asked to become his disciple.

The teacher said: 'You are not yet ready.'

Since the young man was insistent, the sage said: 'Very well, I will teach you something. I am going on a pilgrimage to Mecca. Come with me.'

The disciple was overjoyed.

'Since we are travelling companions,' said the teacher, 'one must lead, and the other obey. Choose your role.'

'I shall follow, you lead,' said the disciple.

'I shall lead, if you know how to follow,' said the master.

The journey started. While they were resting one night in the desert of the Hejaz, it started to rain. The master got up and held a covering over the disciple, protecting him.

'But this is what *I* should be doing for you,' said the disciple.

'I command you to allow me to protect you thus,' said the sage.

When it was day the young man said: 'Now it is a new day. Let *me* be the leader, and you follow me.' The master agreed.

'I shall now collect brushwood, to make a fire,' said the youth.

'You may do no such thing; I shall collect it,' said the sage.

'I command you to sit there while I collect the brushwood!' said the young man.

'You may do no such thing,' said the teacher; 'for it is not in accordance with the requirements of discipleship for the follower to allow himself to be served by the leader.'

And so, on every occasion, the Master showed the student what discipleship really meant, by demonstration.

They parted at the gate of the Holy City. Seeing the sage later, the young man could not meet his eyes.

'That which you have learned', said the older man, 'is something of the nature of discipleship.'

∞

Ibrahim Khawwas (The Palm Weaver) defined the Sufi Path as: 'Allow what is done for you to be done for you. Do for yourself that which you have to do for yourself.'

This story underlines in a dramatic manner the difference between what the would-be disciple *thinks* his relationship with a teaching master should be; and what it actually would be.

Khawwas was one of the great early masters, and this journey is quoted in Hujwiri's *Revelation of the Veiled*, the oldest extant compendium of Sufism in Persian.

The Initiation of Malik Dinar

AFTER many years' study of philosophical subjects, Malik Dinar felt that the time had come to travel in search of knowledge. 'I will go,' he said to himself, 'seeking the Hidden Teacher, who is also said to be within my uttermost self.'

Walking out of his house with only a few dates for provision, he came presently upon a dervish plodding along the dusty road. He fell into step alongside him, in silence for a time.

Finally the dervish spoke. 'Who are you and where are you going?'

'I am Dinar, and I have started to journey in search of the Hidden Teacher.'

'I am El-Malik El-Fatih, and I will walk with you,' said the dervish.

'Can you help me to find the Teacher?' asked Dinar.

'Can I help you, can you help me?' asked Fatih, in the irritating manner of dervishes everywhere; 'the Hidden Teacher, so they say, is in a man's self. How he finds him depends upon what use he makes of experience. This is something only partly conveyed by a companion.'

Presently they came to a tree, which was creaking and swaying. The dervish stopped. 'The tree is saying,' he said after a moment: "Something is hurting me, stop awhile and take it out of my side so that I may find repose." '

'I am in too much of a hurry,' replied Dinar. 'And how can a tree talk, anyway?' They went on their way.

After a few miles the dervish said, 'When we were near the tree I thought that I smelt honey. Perhaps it was a wild-bees' hive which had been built in its bole.'

'If that is true,' said Dinar, 'let us hurry back, so that we may collect the honey, which we could eat, and sell some for the journey.'

'As you wish,' said the dervish.

When they arrived back at the tree, however, they saw some other travellers collecting an enormous quantity of honey. 'What luck we have had!' these men said. 'This is enough honey to feed a city. We poor pilgrims can now become merchants: our future is assured.'

Dinar and Fatih went on their way.

Presently they came to a mountain on whose slopes they heard a humming. The dervish put his ear to the ground. Then he said: 'Below us there are millions of ants, building a colony. This humming is a concerted plea for help. In ant-language it says: "Help us, help us. We are excavating, but have come across strange rocks which bar our progress. Help dig them away." Should we stop and help, or do you want to hasten ahead?'

'Ants and rocks are not our business, brother,' said Dinar, 'because I, for one, am seeking my Teacher.'

'Very well, brother,' said the dervish. 'Yet they do say that all things are connected, and this may have a certain connection with us.'

Dinar took no notice of the older man's mumblings, and so they went their way.

The pair stopped for the night, and Dinar found that he had lost his knife. 'I must have dropped it near the ant-hill,' he said. Next morning they retraced their way.

When they arrived back at the ant-hill, they could find no sign of Dinar's knife. Instead they saw a group of people, covered in mud, resting beside a pile of gold coins. 'These', said the people, 'are a hidden hoard which we have just dug up. We were on the road when a frail old dervish called to us: "Dig at this spot and you will find that which is rocks to some but gold to others." '

Dinar cursed his luck. 'If we had only stopped,' he said, 'you and I would both have been rich last night, O Dervish.' The other party said: 'This dervish with you, stranger, looks strangely like the one whom we saw last night.'

'All dervishes look very much alike,' said Fatih. And they went their respective ways.

Dinar and Fatih continued their travels, and some days later they came to a beautiful river-bank. The Dervish stopped and as they sat waiting for the ferry a fish rose several times to the surface and mouthed at them.

'This fish', said the Dervish, 'is sending us a message. It says: "I have swallowed a stone. Catch me and give me a certain herb to eat. Then I will be able to bring it up, and will thus find relief. Travellers, have mercy!" '

At that moment the ferry-boat appeared and Dinar, impatient to get ahead, pushed the dervish into it. The boatman was grateful for the copper which they were able to give him, and Fatih and Dinar slept well that night on the opposite bank, where a teahouse for travellers had been placed by a charitable soul.

In the morning they were sipping their tea when the ferryman appeared. Last night had been his most fortunate one, he said; the pilgrims had brought him luck. He kissed the hands of the vener-able dervish, to take his blessing. 'You deserve it all, my son,' said Fatih.

The ferryman was now rich: and this was how it had happened. He was about to go home at his usual time, but he had seen the pair on the opposite bank and resolved to make one more trip, although they looked poor, for the 'baraka', the blessing of helping the traveller. When he was about to put away his boat he saw the fish, which had thrown itself on the bank. It was apparently trying to swallow a piece of plant. The fisherman put the plant into its mouth. The fish threw up a stone and flopped back into the water. The stone was a huge and flawless diamond of incalculable value and brilliance.

'You are a devil!' shouted the infuriated Dinar to the dervish Fatih. 'You knew about all three treasures by means of some hidden perception, yet you did not tell me at the time. Is *that* true com-panionship? Formerly, my ill-luck was strong enough: but without you I would not even have known of the possibilities hidden in trees, ant-hills and fish—of all things!'

No sooner had he said these words than he felt as though a mighty wind were sweeping through his very soul. And then he knew that the very reverse of what he had said was the truth.

The dervish, whose name means the Victorious King, touched Dinar lightly on the shoulder, and smiled. 'Now, brother, you will find that you can learn by experience. I am he who is at the command of the Hidden Teacher.'

When Dinar dared to look up, he saw his Teacher walking down the road with a small band of travellers, who were arguing about the perils of the journey ahead of them.

Today the name of Malik Dinar is numbered among the foremost of the dervishes, companion and exemplar, the Man who Arrived.

෴

Malik Dinar was one of the early classical masters.

The Victorious King of the story is an incarnation of the 'higher functions of the mind', called by Rumi 'The Human Spirit', which man must cultivate before he can function in an enlightened manner.

This version is that of Emir el-Arifin.

The Idiot and the Browsing Camel

AN IDIOT looked at a browsing camel. He said to it: 'Your appearance is awry. Why is this so?'

The camel replied: 'In judging the impression made, you are attributing a fault to that which shaped the form. Be aware of this! Do not consider my crooked appearance a fault.

'Get away from me, by the shortest route. My appearance is thus for function, for a reason. The bow needs the bentness as well as the straightness of the bowstring.

'Fool, begone! An ass's perception goes with an ass's nature.'

Maulana Majdud, known as Hakim Sanai the Illuminated Reviving Sage of Ghazna, writes extensively on the unreliability of subjective impressions and conditioned judgments.

One of his sayings is: 'In the distorting mirror of your mind, an angel can seem to have a devil's face.'

This parable is from his *Walled Garden of Truth*, which was written about 1130.

The Three Jewelled Rings

THERE was once a wise and very rich man who had a son. He said to him: 'My son, here is a jewelled ring. Keep it as a sign that you are a successor of mine, and pass it down to your posterity. It is of value, of fine appearance, and it has the added capacity of opening a certain door to wealth.'

Some years later he had another son. When he was old enough, the wise man gave him another ring, with the same advice.

The same thing happened in the case of his third and last son.

When the Ancient had died and the sons grew up, one after the other, each claimed primacy for himself because of his possession of one of the rings. Nobody could tell for certain which was the most valuable.

Each son gained his adherents, all claiming a greater value or beauty for *his* own ring.

But the curious thing was that the 'door to wealth' remained shut for the possessors of the keys and even their closest supporters. They were all too preoccupied with the problem of precedence, the possession of the ring, its value and appearance.

Only a few looked for the door to the treasury of the Ancient. But the rings had a magical quality, too. Although they were keys. they were not used directly in opening the door to the treasury, It was sufficient to look upon them without contention or too much attachment to one or the other of their qualities. When this had been done, the people who had looked were able to tell where the treasury was, and could open it merely by reproducing the outline of the ring. The treasuries had another quality, too: they were inexhaustible.

Meanwhile the partisans of the three rings repeated the tale of their ancestor about the merits of the rings, each in a slightly different way.

The first community thought that they had already found the treasure.

The second thought that it was allegorical.

The third transferred the possibility of the opening of the door to a distant and remotely imagined future time.

∞

This tale, supposed by some to refer to the three religions of Judaism, Christianity and Islam, appears in slightly differing forms both in the *Gesta Romanorum* and in the *Decameron* of Boccacio.

The above version is said to be the answer of one of the Suhrawardi Sufi masters, when asked about the relative merits of various religions. Some commentators have found in it the origin of Swift's *Tale of a Tub*.

It is also known as the Declaration of the Guide of the Royal Secret.

The Man with the Inexplicable Life

THERE was once a man named Mojud. He lived in a town where he had obtained a post as a small official, and it seemed likely that he would end his days as Inspector of Weights and Measures.

One day when he was walking through the gardens of an ancient building near his home Khidr, the mysterious Guide of the Sufis, appeared to him, dressed in shimmering green. Khidr said: 'Man of bright prospects! Leave your work and meet me at the riverside in three days' time.' Then he disappeared.

Mojud went to his superior in trepidation and said that he had to leave. Everyone in the town soon heard of this and they said: 'Poor Mojud! He has gone mad.' But, as there were many candidates for his job, they soon forgot him.

On the appointed day, Mojud met Khidr, who said to him: 'Tear your clothes and throw yourself into the stream. Perhaps someone will save you.'

Mojud did so, even though he wondered if he were mad.

Since he could swim, he did not drown, but drifted a long way before a fisherman hauled him into his boat, saying, 'Foolish man! The current is strong. What are you trying to do?'

Mojud said: 'I do not really know.'

'You are mad,' said the fisherman, 'but I will take you into my reed-hut by the river yonder, and we shall see what can be done for you.'

When he discovered that Mojud was well-spoken, he learned from him how to read and write. In exchange Mojud was given food and helped the fisherman with his work. After a few months, Khidr again appeared, this time at the foot of Mojud's bed, and said: 'Get up now and leave this fisherman. You will be provided for.'

Mojud immediately quit the hut, dressed as a fisherman, and wandered about until he came to a highway. As dawn was breaking he saw a farmer on a donkey on his way to market. 'Do you seek work?' asked the farmer. 'Because I need a man to help me to bring back some purchases.'

Mojud followed him. He worked for the farmer for nearly two years, by which time he had learned a great deal about agriculture but little else.

One afternoon when he was baling wool, Khidr appeared to him and said: 'Leave that work, walk to the city of Mosul, and use your savings to become a skin merchant.'

Mojud obeyed.

In Mosul he became known as a skin merchant, never seeing Khidr while he plied his trade for three years. He had saved quite a large sum of money, and was thinking of buying a house, when Khidr appeared and said: 'Give me your money, walk out of this town as far as distant Samarkand, and work for a grocer there.'
Mojud did so.

Presently he began to show undoubted signs of illumination. He healed the sick, served his fellow men in the shop and during his spare time, and his knowledge of the mysteries became deeper and deeper.

Clerics, philosophers and others visited him and asked: 'Under whom did you study?'

'It is difficult to say,' said Mojud.

His disciples asked: 'How did you start your career?'

He said: 'As a small official.'

'And you gave it up to devote yourself to self-mortification?'

'No, I just gave it up.'

They did not understand him.

People approached him to write the story of his life.

'What have you been in your life?' they asked.

'I jumped into a river, became a fisherman, then walked out of his reed-hut in the middle of one night. After that, I became a farmhand. While I was baling wool, I changed and went to Mosul, where I became a skin merchant. I saved some money there, but gave it away. Then I walked to Samarkand where I worked for a grocer. And this is where I am now.'

'But this inexplicable behaviour throws no light upon your strange gifts and wonderful examples,' said the biographers.

'That is so,' said Mojud.

So the biographers constructed for Mojud a wonderful and exciting history; because all saints must have their story, and the story must be in accordance with the appetite of the listener, not with the realities of the life.

And nobody is allowed to speak of Khidr directly. That is why this story is not true. It is a representation of a life. This is the real life of one of the greatest Sufis.

∞

Sheikh Ali Farmadhi (died 1078) regarded this tale as important in illustrating the Sufi belief that the 'invisible world' is at all times, at various places, interpenetrating ordinary reality.

Things, he says, which we take to be inexplicable are in fact due to this intervention. Furthermore, people do not recognize the participation of this 'world' in our own, because they believe that they know the real cause of events. They do not. It is only when they can hold in their mind the possibility of another dimension sometimes impinging upon the ordinary experiences that this dimension can become available to them.

The Sheikh is the tenth Sheikh and teaching Master of the Khwajagan ('masters'), later to be known as the Naqshbandi Way.

This version is from the seventeenth-century manuscript of Lala Anwar, *Hikayat-i-Abdalan* ('Tales of the Transformed Ones').

The Man Whose Time was Wrong

ONCE upon a time there was a rich merchant who lived in Baghdad. He had a substantial house, large and small properties and dhows which sailed to the Indies with rich cargoes. He had gained these things partly through inheritance, partly through his own efforts, exercised at the right time and place, partly through the benevolent advice and direction of the King of the West, as the Sultan of Cordoba was called at that time.

Then something went wrong. A cruel oppressor seized the land and houses. Ships which had gone to the Indies foundered in typhoons, disaster struck his house and his family. Even his close friends seemed to have lost their power to be in a true harmony with him, although both he and they wanted to have the right kind of social relationship.

The merchant decided to journey to Spain to see his former patron, and he set off across the Western Desert. On the way one accident after another overtook him. His donkey died; he was captured by bandits and sold into slavery, from which he escaped only with the greatest difficulty; his face was tanned by the sun until it was like leather; rough villagers drove him away from their doors. Here and there a dervish gave him a morsel of food and a rag to cover himself. Sometimes he was able to scoop a little fresh water from a pool, but more often than not it was brackish.

Ultimately he reached the entrance of the palace of the King of the West.

Even here he had the greatest difficulty in gaining entry. Soldiers pushed him away with the hafts of their spears, chamberlains refused to talk to him. He was put to work as a minor employee at the Court until he could earn enough to buy a dress suitable to wear when applying to the Master of Ceremonies for admission to the Royal Presence.

But he remembered that he was near to the presence of the king, and the recollection of the Sultan's kindness to him long ago was still in his mind. Because, however, he had been so long in his state of poverty and distress, his manners had suffered, and the Master of Ceremonies decided that he would have to take a course in behaviour and self-discipline before he could allow him to be presented at Court.

All this the merchant endured until, three years after he quit Baghdad, he was shown into the audience hall.

The king recognized him at once, asked him how he was, and bade him sit in a place of honour beside him.

'Your Majesty,' said the merchant, 'I have suffered most terribly these past years. My lands were usurped, my patrimony expropriated, my ships were lost and with them all my capital. For three years I have battled against hunger, bandits, the desert, people whose language I did not understand. Here I am, to throw myself upon Your Majesty's mercy.'

The king turned to the Chamberlain. 'Give him a hundred sheep, make him a Royal Shepherd, send him up yonder mountain, and let him get on with his work.'

Slightly subdued because the king's generosity seemed less than he had hoped for, the merchant withdrew, after the customary salutation.

No sooner had he reached the scanty pasturage with his sheep than a plague struck them, and they all died. He returned to the Court.

'How are your sheep?' asked the king.

'Your Majesty, they died as soon as I got them to their pasture.'

The king made a sign and decreed: 'Give this man fifty sheep, and let him tend them until further notice.'

Feeling ashamed and distraught, the shepherd took the fifty animals to the mountainside. They started to nibble the grass well enough, but suddenly a couple of wild dogs appeared and chased them over a precipice and they were all killed.

The merchant, greatly sorrowing, returned to the king and told him his story.

'Very well,' said the king, 'you may now take twenty-five sheep and continue as before.'

With almost no hope left in his heart, and feeling distraught beyond measure because he did not feel himself to be a shepherd in any sense of the word, the merchant took his sheep to their pasture. As soon as he got them there he found that the ewes all gave birth to twins, nearly doubling his flock. Then, again, twins were born. These new sheep were fat and well-fleeced and made excellent eating. The merchant found that, by selling some of the sheep and buying others, the ones which he bought, at first so skimpy and small, grew strong and healthy, and resembled the amazing new breed which he was rearing. After three years he was able to return to the Court, splendidly attired, with his report of the way in which the sheep had prospered during his stewardship. He was immediately admitted to the presence of the king.

'Are you now a successful shepherd?' the monarch asked. 'Yes indeed, Your Majesty. In an incomprehensible way my luck turned and I can say that nothing has gone wrong—although I still have little taste for raising sheep.'

'Very well,' said the king. 'Yonder is the kingdom of Seville, whose throne is in my gift. Go, and let it be known that I make you king of Seville.' And he touched him on the shoulder with the ceremonial axe.

The merchant could not restrain himself and burst out: 'But why did you not make me a king when I first came to you? Were you testing my patience, already stretched almost to breaking point? Or was this to teach me something?'

The king laughed. 'Let us just say that, on that day when you took the hundred sheep up the mountain and lost them, had you taken control of the kingdom of Seville, there would not have been one stone standing on top of another there today.'

Abdul-Qadir of Gilan was born in the eleventh century near the southern shores of the Caspian Sea. Because of his descent from Hasan, grandson of Mohammed, he is known as *Sayedna* — 'Our Prince'. The powerful Qadiri Order is named after him. He is reputed to have displayed paranormal powers from childhood, studied at Baghdad and spent a great deal of his time in trying to establish free public education. Shahabudin Suhrawardi, one of the greatest Sufi writers, who wrote the *Gifts of Deep Knowledge*, was his disciple. Innumerable wonders are related about both of these men.

He had a large number of Jewish and Christian, as well as Moslem, disciples. He died in 1166. As he lay on his deathbed a mysterious Arab appeared with a letter. In it was written: 'This is a letter from the Lover to his beloved. Every person and every animal has to taste death.' His shrine is at Baghdad.

Since Abdul Qadir is widely venerated as a saint, numerous hagiographies dealing with his life are current in the East. They are full of wonders and strange ideas.

Hiyat-i-Hazrat ('Life of the Presence'), which is one such book, begins like this:

'His appearance was formidable. One day only one disciple dared to ask a question. This was: "Can you not give us power to improve the earth and the lot of the people of the earth?" His brow darkened, and he said: "I will do better: I will give this power to your descendants, because as yet there is no hope of such improvement being made on a large enough scale. The devices do not yet exist. You shall be rewarded; and they shall have the reward of their efforts and of your aspiration."'

A similar sense of chronology is displayed in 'The Man Whose Time was Wrong'.

Maruf the Cobbler

ONCE upon a time in the city of Cairo lived a cobbler named Maruf and his wife Fatima. This hag treated him so badly, repaying every good action with a bad one, that Maruf began to look upon her as the embodiment of the inexplicable contrariness of the world.

Bowed down with a sense of real injustice, driven to the last extremity of despair, he fled to a ruined monastery near the city where he plunged himself in prayer and supplication, calling out incessantly: 'Lord, I beg of thee to send me a means of release, so that I may travel an immense distance from this place, to find safety and hope.'

This he continued to do for several hours when an amazing thing happened. A being of great height and strange appearance seemed to pass straight through the wall in front of him, after the manner attributed to the powers of the *Abdal*, the 'Changed Ones', who are human beings who have attained powers far beyond those of ordinary men.

'I am the Abdel-Makan, the Servant of this Place,' said the apparition. 'What do you ask from me?'

Maruf told him all his problems. The Changed One had Maruf mount his back, and they flew through the air for several hours at an unparalleled speed. Maruf found himself as daylight dawned in a far city on the borders of China, a rich and beautiful place.

One of the citizens stopped him in the street, and asked him who he was. When Maruf told him, and tried to explain the manner of his coming, a crowd of jeering louts collected; throwing sticks and stones, they accused him of being mad or else an impostor of some kind.

The mob was still handling the unfortunate cobbler roughly when a merchant rode up and dispersed them, saying, 'Have shame! A stranger is a guest, bound to us by the sacred bonds of hospitality and worthy of our protection.' His name was Ali.

Ali explained to his friend how he had progressed from rags to riches in this strange city of Ikhtiyar. The merchants there, it seemed, were generally more inclined than other folk to take a man at his word. If he was poor, they would not give him much of a chance in life, because they considered that man was poor because he had to be so. If, on the other hand, a man was said to be rich, they would give him consideration, credit and honour.

Ali had discovered this fact. He had therefore gone to several rich merchants of the town and asked them for loans, saying that a caravan of his had not yet arrived. The loans were made, Ali multiplied the money by trading in the great bazaars, and he had been able to return the original capital and actually to make himself rich.

He advised Maruf to do the same.

Thus it was that Maruf, dressed by his friend in a sumptuous robe, went and borrowed from one merchant after another. The only difference was that, because of his charitable disposition, Maruf gave the money away to beggars. His caravan, after months of waiting, showed no signs of arriving, and Maruf was doing no business, but his charity increased, for people vied with each other to give money on loan to a man who immediately spent it on charity. In this way, they thought, they would both get their loans back when the caravan arrived and also participate, at one remove, in the blessing inseparable from acts of benevolence.

As time passed, however, the merchants began to wonder whether Maruf was after all an impostor. They went to the king of the city to complain. The king called Maruf before him.

The king was in two minds about Maruf and resolved to test him. He had a valuable jewel, which he decided to present to the merchant Maruf, to see whether he realized its value or not. If he did, the king—who was a greedy man—would give his daughter in marriage to Maruf. If he did not, he would be thrown in jail.

Maruf presented himself at Court, and the jewel was placed in his hands. 'This is for you, good Maruf,' said the king. 'But tell me, why do you not pay your debts?'

'Because, your Majesty, my caravan of priceless things has still not arrived. As for this jewel, I think it better for your Majesty to keep it, for it is worthless compared to the really valuable jewels which I have in my caravan.'

Overcome by greed the king dismissed Maruf and sent a message to the representative of the merchants to hold their peace. He resolved to marry the princess to the merchant, in spite of the Grand Wazir's opposition. The Wazir said that Maruf was a manifest liar. The king, however, remembered that the Wazir had been asking for the princess's hand for years, and attributed his advice to prejudice.

Maruf, when he was told that the king would bestow his daughter upon him, merely said to the Wazir, 'Tell his Majesty that until my caravan arrives, loaded with priceless jewels and the like, I cannot make due provision for a princess-wife, and hence I suggest the marriage be postponed.'

Told of this attitude, the king immediately opened his treasury to Maruf, so that he could choose whatever he needed for the setting up of a suitable way of life and for gifts consonant with the rank of a royal son-in-law.

Never was such a marriage seen in that or any other country Not only were alms distributed by the handful of jewels, but everyone who even heard of the wedding was given a lavish present. The celebrations lasted for forty days in unprecedented magnificence.

When they were at last alone, Maruf said to his bride: 'I have already taken so much from your father that I am troubled,' because he had to account for his being somewhat sore at heart. 'Think nothing of it,' said the princess, 'for when your caravan arrives, all will be well.'

Meanwhile the Wazir renewed his agitation with the king to investigate Maruf's real position. They decided to seek the princess's help, and she agreed to find out, at an opportune moment, the real truth of the matter.

As they lay in one another's arms, the princess that night asked her husband to explain the mystery of the missing caravan. Maruf had just that very day told his friend Ali that he indeed did have a caravan of priceless worth. But now he decided to speak the truth. 'There is no caravan,' he said, 'and although the Wazir is right, his words are due to his greed. Your father, too, gave you to me because of his own greed. Why did you yourself consent to marry me?'

'You are my husband,' replied the princess, 'and I will never disgrace you. Take these fifty thousand gold pieces, flee the country, send me a message from safety, where I will join you in due course. Meanwhile, leave me to attend to the court situation.' Dressed as a slave, Maruf fled in the dead of night.

Now, when the king and the Wazir called the Princess Dunia to them for her report, she said:

'Respected Father and Most Worthy Wazir, I was about to broach the question with my husband Maruf last night, when a strange thing happened.'

'What was that?' they exclaimed together.

'Ten Mamelukes, dressed most magnificently, arrived beneath the palace window, carrying a letter from the chief of Maruf's caravan. The letter said that they had been delayed because of an attack by numerous bedouins, fifty of the guards out of the five hundred were killed, and a quantity of the merchandise, two hundred camel-loads, was carried off.'

'And what did Maruf say?'

'He said very little. Two hundred loads and fifty lives were nothing, he thought. But he at once rode off to meet the caravan and bring it back to us.'

Thus the Princess bought time.

As for Maruf, he rode hard, not knowing where, until he came to a peasant ploughing a small strip of land. To him he gave greeting, and the peasant said, out of the goodness of his heart:

'Be a guest of mine, Great Slave of the King's Majesty. I will bring you some food to share with me.'

He hurried off, and Maruf, touched by his kindness, decided to continue with the man's ploughing, as a contribution to his welfare. He had not made many furrows when the plough struck a stone. When he pulled it away, a flight of steps leading into the ground was revealed. Below was a huge chamber, filled with innumerable treasures.

In a crystal box was a ring, which Maruf picked out and rubbed. Instantly a strange apparition materialized, crying: 'Here am I, thy servant, my Lord.'

Maruf discovered that this Jinn was known as Father of Happiness, and that he was one of the most powerful commanders of the Jinn, and that the treasure had belonged to the ancient king Shaddad, son of Aad. The Father of Happiness was now the slave of Maruf.

The cobbler ordered the treasure to be taken to the surface of the ground. Then it was loaded on camels and mules and horses, materialized by the Jinn. Every kind of precious material was also produced by the other Jinns who served the Father of Happiness, and the caravan was soon ready to depart.

The peasant returned with a little barley and pulse. Now that he saw Maruf and his treasures he imagined that this must be a king. Maruf gave him some gold and told him to claim a greater reward later. Accepting the peasant's hospitality, he ate only pulse and barley.

Maruf sent the Jinns (for such were the men and animals in disguise) ahead to the city of his father-in-law. When they arrived, the king attacked the Wazir for his having ever suggested that Maruf was a pauper. When the Princess heard that a resplendent caravan had arrived, belonging to Maruf, she did not know what the truth was. She suspected that Maruf had said that he had lied in order to test her loyalty.

Maruf's friend Ali, for his part, assumed that this great caravan was the work of the princess, who must surely in some way have contrived to save her husband's name and life.

All the merchants who had lent money to Maruf and had wondered at his generosity with it, were now even more amazed at the amount of gold, jewels and gifts which he was distributing to the poor and needy.

But the Wazir was still suspicious. No merchant was ever known to act in this way, he told the king; and he proposed a plot. He lured Maruf into a garden, plied him with music and wine: and in his drunkenness Maruf confessed the truth. The Wazir then borrowed the magical ring from the unresisting Maruf, made the Jinn appear, and ordered him to spirit Maruf away into the farthest desert. Reviling him for revealing the precious secret, the Jinn willingly snatched up Maruf and threw him down in the Hadhramaut wilderness. Now the Wazir commanded the Jinn to take his master the king and hurl him down together with Maruf. The Wazir seized power and even tried to seduce the princess.

The princess, however, when the Wazir came to her, got possession of the ring from his finger, rubbed it and had the Jinn take the minister away in chains. In one hour the Jinn had brought back the king and Maruf to the palace. The Wazir was put to death for his treachery, and Maruf became the prime minister in his stead.

They lived happily together thereafter. The king died and Maruf succeeded him. He now had a son. The princess retained possession of the ring. Now she became ill and, handing over the care of the child and the ring to Maruf, she died, warning him to take equal care of each.

Not long afterwards, King Maruf was lying in bed when he awoke with a start. Beside him was none other than his first wife, the hideous Fatima, transported there by magical means. She explained what had befallen her.

When Maruf disappeared she repented and became a beggar. Life was hard, and she was reduced to the utmost extremity of suffering. One day while she was lying down trying to sleep, she cried out in her distress, when a Jinn appeared and told her about the adventures of Maruf since they had last met. She asked him to take her to Ikhtiyar, and she had been brought there with the speed of light.

She was now most contrite, and Maruf agreed to take her back as his wife, warning her that he was now a king and master of a magical ring, whose servitor was the great Jinn, Father of

167

Happiness. Humbly, she thanked him, and took her place as the queen. But she hated the little prince.

Now, at night, Maruf used to take off his magical ring. Fatima knew this, and before long crept into his bedroom and stole it. The little boy, however, had followed her, and when he saw her steal the ring, he drew his tiny sword and killed the hag, fearful of the exercise of her new power.

Thus did the false Fatima find her grave at the place of her greatest honour. Now Maruf called the honest peasant who had been the instrument of his salvation and made him prime minister. He married the peasant's daughter. And thereafter all lived in happiness and success.

တတ

Like various other dervish tales, this one appears in the *Arabian Nights*. Unlike most Sufi allegories, it is not found in poetic form. Again, unlike most except for the Mulla Nasrudin cycle, it is sometimes performed in Chaikhanas (tea-houses) as a drama.

It has no moral, as people in the West are accustomed to them, but it stresses certain cause-and-effect relationships which are a marked feature of some Sufi literature.

Wisdom for Sale

A MAN named Saifulmuluk spent half of his life in seeking truth. He read all the books on ancient wisdom which he could find. He travelled to every known and unknown country to hear what spiritual teachers had to say. He spent the days in working and the nights in contemplation of the Great Mysteries.

One day he heard of yet another teacher, the great poet Ansari, who lived in the city of Herat. Bending his steps thither he arrived at the door of the sage. On it he saw written, contrary to his expectation, a strange announcement: 'Knowledge is Sold Here.'

'This must be a mistake, or else a deliberate attempt to dissuade the idle curiosity-seeker,' he said to himself, 'for I have never before heard it said that knowledge can be bought or sold.' So he went into the house.

Sitting in the inner courtyard was Ansari himself, bent with age and writing a poem. 'Have you come to buy knowledge?' he asked. Saifulmuluk nodded. Ansari told him to produce as much money as he had. Saifulmuluk took out all his money, amounting to a hundred pieces of silver.

'For this much', said Ansari, 'you can have three pieces of advice.'

'Do you really mean that?' asked Saifulmuluk. 'Why do you need money, if you are a humble and dedicated man?'

'We live in the world, surrounded by its material facts,' said the sage, 'and with the knowledge that I have I gain great new responsibilities. Because I know certain things that others do not, I have to spend money, among other things, to be of service where a kind word or the exercise of "baraka" is not indicated.'

He took the silver and said, 'Listen well.

'The first piece of advice is: "A small cloud signals danger." '

'But is this knowledge?' asked Saifulmuluk. 'It does not seem to tell me much about the nature of ultimate truth, or about man's place in the world.'

'If you are going to interrupt me', said the sage, 'you can take your money back and go away. What is the use of knowledge about man's place in the world if that man is dead?'

Saifulmuluk was silenced, and he waited for the next piece of advice.

'The second piece of advice is: "If you can find a bird, a cat and a dog in one place, get hold of them and look after them until the end."'

'This is curious advice,' thought Saifulmuluk, 'but perhaps it has an inner metaphysical meaning which will become manifest to me if I meditate upon it long enough.'

So he held his peace until the sage brought forth the last piece of advice:

'When you have experienced certain things which seem irrelevant, keeping faith with the foregoing advice, then and only then will a door open for you. Enter that door.'

Saifulmuluk wanted to stay to study under this baffling sage, but Ansari sent him away, rather roughly.

He continued his wanderings, and went to Kashmir to study under a teacher there. When he was travelling through central Asia again, he reached the market-place of Bokhara during an auction sale. A man was leading away a cat, a bird and a dog which he had just bought. 'If I had not tarried so long in Kashmir,' thought Saifulmuluk, 'I would have been able to buy these animals, because they certainly are a part of my destiny.'

Then he started to worry, because although he had seen the bird, the cat and the dog, he had not yet seen the small cloud. Everything seemed to be going wrong. The only thing that saved him was looking through one of his notebooks in which he had recorded, though not remembered, the advice of an ancient sage: 'Things happen in succession. Man imagines this succession to be of a certain kind. But it sometimes is another kind of succession.'

Then he realized that, although the three animals had been

bought at an auction, Ansari had not actually told him to buy them at an auction. He had not remembered the words of the advice, which had been, 'If you can find a bird, a cat and a dog in one place, get hold of them, and look after them until the end.'

So he started to trace the buyer of the animals, to see whether they were still 'in one place'.

After many inquiries, he found out that the man was called Ashikikhuda, and that he had only bought the animals to save them the pain of being cooped up in the auctioneer's rooms, where they had been for several weeks, awaiting a buyer. They were still 'in one place' and Ashikikhuda was glad to sell them to Saifulmuluk.

He settled in Bokhara, because it was not practicable to continue journeying with the animals. Every day he went out to work in a wool-spinning factory, returning in the evening with food for the animals which he had bought from his day's earnings. Time passed, three years.

One day when he had become a master-spinner, and was living as a respected member of the community with his animals, he walked to the outskirts of the town and saw what seemed to be a tiny cloud, hovering almost on the horizon. It was such a strange-looking cloud that his memory was jogged, and the First Piece of Advice came into his consciousness, very sharply:

'A small cloud signals danger.'

Saifulmuluk returned immediately to his house, collected his animals and started to flee westwards. He arrived in Isfahan almost penniless. Some days later he learned that the cloud which he had seen was the dust of a conquering horde, which had captured Bokhara and slain all its inhabitants.

And the words of Ansari came into his mind: 'What is the use of knowledge about man's place in the world if that man is dead?'

The people of Isfahan were not enamoured of animals, wool-spinners nor strangers, and Saifulmuluk was before long reduced to extreme poverty. He threw himself down on the ground and cried: 'O Succession of Saints! O Holy Ones! Ye who have been Changed! Come you to my aid, for I am reduced to a state in which my own efforts no longer yield sustenance, and my animals are suffering hunger and thirst.'

As he lay there, between sleeping and waking, his stomach gnawed by hunger, and having resigned himself to the guidance of his fate, he saw a vision of something as clearly as if it were there. It was a picture of a golden ring, set with a changing lighted stone, which flashed fire, glowed like the phosphorescent sea, and in its depths gave off green lights.

A voice, or so it seemed to be, said: 'This is the golden crown of the ages, the Samir of Truth, the very Ring of King Solomon, the son of David, upon whose name be peace, whose secrets are to be preserved.'

Looking around him, he saw that the ring was rolling into a crevice in the ground. It seemed as though he was beside a stream, under a tree, near a curiously-shaped boulder.

In the morning, rested and more able to bear his hunger, Saifulmuluk started to wander around the periphery of Isfahan. Then as he had half-expected for some reason, he saw the stream, the tree and the rock. Under the rock there was a crevice. In the crevice, into which he interposed a stick, was the ring which he had already seen in the curious way related above.

Washing the ring in the water, Saifulmuluk exclaimed: 'If this is truly the Ring of the Great Solomon, upon whom be the Salute, grant me, Spirit of the Ring, a worthy end to my difficulties.'

Suddenly it was as if the earth shook, and as if a voice like a whirlwind was echoing in his ears: 'Across the centuries, good Saifulmuluk, we bid you peace. You are the inheritor of the power of Solomon the son of David, upon whom be peace, Master of the Jinns and Men, I am the Slave of the Ring. Command me, Master Saifulmuluk, Master!'

'Bring the animals here, and food for them,' said Saifulmuluk at once, not forgetting to add: 'In the Great Name and in the Name of Solomon, our Master, Commander of the Jinns and Men, upon him be the Salute!'

Almost before he had finished saying this, there were the animals and each had set before him the necessary food, that which he liked best.

Then he rubbed the ring, and the Spirit of the Ring again answered him, like a rushing in the ears.

'Command me, and whatever you desire shall be done, save only that which is not to be done, Master of the Ring.'

'Tell me, in the Name of Solomon (peace upon him!) is this the end? For I must look after the welfare of these companions of mine until the end, according to the command of my own master, The Khoja Ansar of Herat.'

'No,' replied the Spirit, 'it is not the end.'

Saifulmuluk stayed at this spot, where he had the Jinn build him a small house and a place for the animals; and he passed his days with them. Every day the Jinn brought them all sufficient for their needs, and passers-by marvelled at the sanctity of Saif-Baba, 'Father Saif', as he was called, 'who lived on nothing, surrounded by tame and wild animals'.

When he was not studying the notes of his travels and contemplating his experiences, Saif-Baba observed the three animals and learned their ways. Each responded to him in its own way. He encouraged their good qualities and discouraged their bad ones, and he often spoke to them about the great Khoja Ansar and the Three Pieces of Advice.

From time to time holy men passed by his habitation, and often they invited him to dispute with them, or to learn their own particular Ways. But he refused, saying, 'I have my task to perform, given me by my teacher.' Then one day he was surprised to find that the cat was speaking to him in a language which he understood. 'Master,' said the cat, 'you have your task, and you must carry it out. But are you not surprised that the time which you call "the end" has not come?'

'I am not really surprised,' said Saif-Baba, 'because for all I know it might last for a hundred years.'

'That is where you are wrong,' said the bird, which was now talking too, 'for you have not learned what you could have learned from the various travellers who have passed this way. You do not realize that although they appear different (as we animals all appear different to you) they were all sent by the source of your teaching, by Khoja Ansar himself, to see whether you had acquired enough insight to follow them.'

'If this is true,' said Saif-Baba, 'which I do not for a moment believe, can you explain to me why it is that a mere cat and a tiny sparrow can tell me things which I, with the miraculous benefits which I have received, cannot see?'

'That is simple,' they both said together. 'It is that you have become so accustomed to looking at things in only one way that your shortcomings are visible even to the most ordinary mind.'

This worried Saif-Baba. 'So I could have found the Door of the Third Piece of Advice long ago, if I had been properly attuned to it?' he asked.

'Yes,' said the dog, joining the discussion. 'The door has opened a dozen times in the past years, but you did not see it. We did, but because we are animals, we could not tell you.'

'Then how can you tell me now?'

'You can understand our speech because you yourself have lately become more human. But you have only one more chance, for age is overcoming you.'

Saif-Baba at first thought: 'This is a hallucination.' Then he thought: 'They have no right to talk to me like this, I am their master and the source of their sustenance.' Then another part of him thought: 'If they are wrong, it does not matter. But if they are right, this is terrible for me. I cannot take a chance.'

So he awaited his opportunity. Months passed. One day a wandering dervish came along and pitched a tent on Saif-Baba's doorstep. He made friends with the animals, and Saif decided to take him into his confidence. 'Away with you!' snapped the dervish, 'I am not interested in your tales of the Master Ansari, your clouds and your seeking and your responsibility to animals, even your magic Ring. Leave me in peace. I know what you *should be* talking about, but I do not know what you *are* talking about.'

Saif-Baba in desperation called the Spirit of the Ring. But the Jinn merely said: 'I am not to tell you those things which are not to be told. But I do know that you are suffering from the disease called "Permanent Hidden Prejudice" which rules your thoughts and makes it difficult for you to progress in the *way*.'

Then Saif-Baba went to the dervish who was sitting on his doorstep and said: 'What should I do, for I feel a responsibility for my animals, and a confusion about myself, and there is no more guidance in my Three Pieces of Advice.'

'You have talked sincerely,' said the dervish, 'and this is a beginning. Hand your animals over to me, and I will tell you the answer.'

'But I do not know you, and you ask too much,' said Saif-Baba. 'How can you ask such a thing? I respect you, but there is still a doubt in my mind.'

'Well spoken,' said the Dervish. 'You have revealed not your concern for your animals, but your own lack of perception about me. If you judge me by emotion or logic, you cannot benefit from me. You still are covetous in some way, maintaining proprietorship over "your" animals. Go away, as sure as my name is Darwaza.'

Now, 'Darwaza' means 'door', and Saif-Baba thought very hard about this. Could this be the 'door' which was foretold by his sheikh, Ansari? 'You may be the "Door" I am seeking, but I am not sure,' he said to the dervish Darwaza. 'Be off with you, you and your speculations,' shouted the dervish. 'Don't you see that the first two pieces of advice were for your mind and that the last piece can be understood only when you perceive it yourself?'

After nearly two more years of confusion and anxiety, Saif-Baba suddenly realized the truth. He called his animals and dismissed them, saying, 'You are on your own now. This is the end.' As he said so, he realized that the animals now had human forms, and that they were transformed. Standing beside him was Darwaza, but his form was now that of the great Khoja Ansar himself. Without saying a word, Ansari opened a door in the tree beside the stream, and as he walked over the threshold Saif-Baba saw written up in letters of gold in a wondrous cavern the answers to the questions about life and death, about mortality and humanity, about knowledge and ignorance, which had plagued him all his life.

'Attachment to externals', said the voice of Ansari, 'has been what has held you back all these years. In some ways because of this, you are too late. Take here the only part of wisdom still open to you.'

തൻ

This story illustrates, among other things, the favourite Sufi theme that Truth is 'trying to manifest itself' among humanity: but that it appears again and again for each man in guises which are difficult of penetration and at first sight may have no connection with each other.

Only the development of a 'special perception' enables man to keep abreast of this unseen process.

The King and the Poor Boy

A MAN alone cannot achieve the traversing of the road of the inner path. You should not try to set out alone, for there must be a guide. That which we call a king is the guide, and he whom we call a poor boy is the Seeker.

It is said that King Mahmud and his army were separated. As he was riding his horse at great speed he saw a small boy on a river bank. The child had cast his net into the water, and seemed greatly sad

'My child,' said the King, 'why are you unhappy? I have never seen anyone in such a state as you.'

The boy answered, 'Your Majesty, I am one of seven children who have no father. We live with our mother in poverty and without support. I come here every day and cast my net for fish, so that I can have something for that night. Unless I catch a fish during the day there is nothing at night.'

'My child,' said the King, 'would you care for me to help in your work?' He agreed, and King Mahmud threw the net which through the royal touch, produced a hundred fish.

༺༻

It is often thought by those who have not studied widely that metaphysical systems either deny the value of things 'of the world' or else promise an abundance of material benefits.

In Sufism, however, the 'good things' gained are not always figurative nor inevitably literal. This parable by the great Faridudin Attar, given in his *Parliament of the Birds*, is used in both the literal and symbolic senses. According to the dervishes, a person may gain material things by the Sufi Way if this is to the advantage of the Way as well as to himself. Equally, he will gain transcendental gifts in accordance with his capacity to use them in the right way.

The Three Teachers and the
Muleteers

SUCH was the repute of Abdul Qadir that mystics of all persuasions used to throng to his reception hall, and the utmost decorum and consideration for the traditional manners uniformly prevailed. These pious men arranged themselves in order of precedence, of age and according to the repute which their teachers had enjoyed and their own precedence in their own communities.

Yet they vied with one another for the attention of the Sultan of the Teachers, Abdul Qadir. His manners were impeccable, and nobody of low intelligence or lack of training was seen at these assemblies.

One day, however, the three sheiks of Khorasan, Iraq and Egypt came to the Dargah, guided by three illiterate muleteers. Their journey from Mecca, where they had been on a pilgrimage, had been plagued by the inelegance and caperings of these men. When they saw the assembly of the Sheikh they were made as happy to think of their release from their companions, as they were by their desire to glimpse the Great Sheikh.

Contrary to the usual practice, the Sheikh came out to meet them. No sign passed between him and the muleteers. Later that night, however, finding their way to their quarters, the three sheikhs glimpsed by accident the Sheikh saying goodnight to the muleteers. As they respectfully left his room, he kissed their hands. The sheikhs were astonished, and realized that these three, and not they, were hidden sheikhs of the dervishes. They followed the muleteers and tried to start a conversation. But the chief muleteer only said: 'Get back to your prayers and mumblings, sheikhs, with your Sufism and your search for truth which has plagued us during thirty-six days' travel. We are simple muleteers and want nothing of that.'

Thus is the different between the hidden Sufis and the superficial ones.

൸

The *Jewish Encyclopedia* and such authorities upon the Hasidic mystics as Martin Buber have noted the affinity between this school and the Spanish Sufis, as far as chronology and similarity of teaching is concerned.

This tale, attributed to the Sufi, Abdul-Qadir of Gilan (1077–1166), is also found ascribed to the life of Hasid Rabbi Elimelech (who died in 1809).

Abdul-Qadir, known as 'King', as also was Elimelech, was the founder of the Qadiri Order of Dervishes.

Bayazid and the Selfish Man

ONE day a man reproached Bayazid, the great mystic of the ninth century, saying that he had fasted and prayed and so on for thirty years and not found the joy which Bayazid described. Bayazid told him that he might continue for three hundred years and still not find it.

'How is that?' asked the would-be illuminate.

'Because your vanity is a barrier to you.'

'Tell me the remedy.'

'The remedy is one which you cannot take.'

'Tell me, nevertheless.'

Bayazid said: 'You must go to the barber and have your (respectable) beard shaved. Remove all your clothes and put a girdle around yourself. Fill a nosebag with walnuts and suspend it from your neck. Go to the market-place and call out: "A walnut will I give to any boy who will strike me on the back of the neck." Then continue on to the justices' session so that they may see you.'

'But I cannot do that; please tell me something else that would do as well.'

'This is the first move, and the only one,' said Bayazid, 'but I had already told you that you would not do it; so you cannot be cured.'

ᴨᴄᴉ

El-Ghazali, in his *Alchemy of Happiness*, seeks with this parable to emphasize his repeated argument that some people, however sincere in seeking truth they may appear to themselves — or even to other people — may in fact be motivated by vanity or self-seeking which imposes a complete barrier to their learning.

The People Who Attain

IMAM EL-GHAZALI relates a tradition from the life of Isa, ibn Maryam.

Isa one day saw some people sitting miserably on a wall, by the roadside.

He asked: 'What is your affliction?'

They said: 'We have become like this through our fear of hell.'

He went on his way, and saw a number of people grouped disconsolately in various postures by the wayside. He said: 'What is your affliction?' They said: 'Desire for Paradise has made us like this.'

He went on his way, until he came to a third group of people. They looked like people who had endured much, but their faces shone with joy.

Isa asked them: 'What has made you like this?'

They answered: 'The Spirit of Truth. We have seen Reality, and this has made us oblivious of lesser goals.'

Isa said: 'These are the people who attain. On the Day of Accounting these are they who will be in the Presence of God.'

ॐ

Those who believe that spiritual advancement depends upon the cultivation of reward and punishment themes alone have often been surprised by this Sufi tradition about Jesus.

Sufis say that only certain people benefit through powerful dwelling upon gain or loss; and that this, in turn, may constitute only a part of anyone's experiences. Those who have studied the methods and effects of conditioning and indoctrination may feel themselves inclined to agree with them.

Formal religionists, of course, do not in many faiths admit that the simple alternatives of good-bad, tension-relaxation, reward-punishment are only parts of a greater system of self-realization.

Wayfarer, Strangeness and Savetime

THREE dervishes met on a lonely road. The first was called Wayfarer, because he always went by the longest route anywhere, due to his respect for tradition. The second was known as Strangeness, because nothing seemed strange to him, though most things he did or even noticed seemed strange to others. The third was named Savetime, because he always thought he could save time, though his ways were often the longest of all.

They became travelling companions. But before long they parted. This was because Wayfarer soon noticed a landmark of which he had heard, and insisted upon taking the road indicated by it. It only led to a ruined city inhabited by lions, because the flourishing metropolis of which he had heard had perished hundreds of years before. He was eaten by the lions, almost in a gulp. A day or two later, Savetime decided to find a shorter way, and fell into a quicksand while trying to cut across country. It was the kind of quicksand which is not dangerous, but it takes months to get out of it.

Strangeness went on alone. Soon he met a man who said to him: 'Dervish, the road is barred ahead because there is a caravanserai inhabited at night by all the wild beasts of the jungle.'

'What do they do during the day?' asked Strangeness.

'I suppose they hunt during the day,' said the man.

'Very well, I shall sleep there during the day and stay awake at night,' said Strangeness.

He approached the caravanserai during daylight, and sure enough he saw there the tracks of numerous animals. He had time to sleep. At nightfall he awoke, and hid himself, to find out why the animals came there.

Presently they all arrived, led by the lion, their King. One by one they saluted the lion and told him tales of things which were known to them and unknown to the human race.

In this way, from his concealment, the dervish learned that no distance away there was a cavern full of jewels, the Treasure of the Karatash, the fabled Black Stone. One of the animals told how in that very caravanserai there was a rat who guarded a treasure of gold pieces, which he could neither spend nor bear to part with, which he brought out at dawn. A third animal explained how a king's daughter might be healed of a madness which had seized her.

This was the strangest story of all, and even Strangeness himself could hardly believe it. In the next valley was a sheep-dog which guarded a large flock. The hair from behind its ears would cure the princess, and nothing less would do. But since no man knew either the remedy or the princess who was soon to be stricken with this malady (he learned), there was no hope of the knowledge being of any use.

Just before dawn the animals dispersed, and Strangeness waited for the rat to appear. Sure enough it came into the middle of the floor, rolling a golden piece. When it had brought the whole hoard out and was counting the pieces, the dervish stepped out of his place of concealment and took the lot. Then he made his way to the Cavern of Karatash and saw the treasure. From there he found the dog and plucked hair from behind its ears. Then he set off on his travels again.

The dervish Strangeness, following strange signs which nobody else would look for, found himself at length at the uttermost confines of the Empire. Entering a strange and quite unfamiliar kingdom, he saw that people were hurrying about with a preoccupied air. He asked them what ailed them. They explained that the daughter of their king had just been stricken with a strange disease, and that nobody could cure her. Strangeness made his way at once to the Palace.

'If you cure my daughter,' said the king, 'you will have half my kingdom, and the rest when I die. If you fail, I shall impale you upon the loftiest minaret.' Strangeness accepted the conditions, and the princess was brought to him. He held the sheepdog's hair in front of her, and immediately she was healed.

And this was how Strangeness became a royal prince and taught his ways to the many respectful people who flocked to learn from him.

One day, however, he was walking in disguise, as was his custom, when he ran into the dervish Savetime, who at first did not recognize him, partly because he was talking all the time and could not spare a moment to identify his old friend. Strangeness, therefore, merely guided Savetime into the Palace, and waited for him to ask questions.

Savetime said: 'How did all this happen? Tell me all, but tell me quickly.'

Strangeness told him, but he could see that Savetime was not taking in the details. He was too impatient. In no time at all, Savetime said: 'I must return there and learn what the animals have to say, so that I can follow the same path as you.'

'I do not advise it,' said Strangeness, 'for you have to learn to interest yourself in Time and in strange signs first.'

'Nonsense,' said Savetime, and was off in a trice, waiting only to borrow a hundred gold pieces for the journey from his fellow-dervish.

When he got to the caravanserai, Savetime found that it was night. Reluctant to wait until the morning to conceal himself from the animals, he walked straight into the main hall, where the lion and tiger immediately leaped upon him and tore him limb from limb.

As for Strangeness, he lived happily ever after.

Found in a dervish manuscript called *Kitab-i-Amu Daria* (The Book of the River Oxus), an annotation makes this tale one of the teaching-stories of Uwais el-Qarni, originator of the Uwaisi ('Solitary') Dervishes.

The theme is that impatience causes one to overlook essential qualities of a situation.

Timur Agha and the Speech of Animals

THERE once was a Turk called Timur Agha, who searched town and city, village and country, for anyone who could teach him the speech of animals and birds. Everywhere he went he made this inquiry, because he knew that the great Najmuddin Kubra had had this power, and he sought one of his lineal disciples in order to profit by this strange lore, the lore of Solomon.

Finally, because he had cultivated the qualities of manliness and generosity, he saved the life of a frail old dervish who was hanging from the webs of a mountain rope-bridge, and who said to him: 'My son, I am Bahaudin the Dervish, and I have read your mind. From henceforward you will know the speech of animals.' Timur promised never to confide the secret to another.

Timur Agha hastened home to his farm. Soon he was able to put his new power to use. An ox and a donkey were talking, in their own manner. The ox said: 'I have to pull a plough, and you only have to go to market. You must be cleverer than I, advise me of a way out of this.'

'All you have to do', said the crafty donkey, 'is to lie down and pretend that you have a terrible stomach-ache. Then the farmer will look after you, because you are a valuable animal. He will allow you to rest and have better food.' But, of course they had been overheard. Timur, when the ox lay down, said in a loud voice: 'I shall send that ox to the butcher tonight unless it is better in half an hour.' And so it was, very much better!

This made Timur laugh, and his wife—who had a curious and sulky disposition—insisted on knowing why he was laughing. Mindful of his promise, he refused to tell her.

The next day they went to market with the farmer walking, his wife sitting on the donkey, and the baby donkey walking behind.

The small donkey brayed, and Timur realized that it was saying to its mother: 'I cannot walk farther, let me get on your back.' The mother answered, in donkey-talk: 'I am carrying the farmer's wife and we are only animals, this is our fate, there is nothing that I can do for you, my child.'

Timur at once made his wife get down from the donkey to allow it to rest. They stopped under a tree. The wife was furious, but Timur just said: 'I think that it is time to rest.'

The donkey said to herself: 'This man knows our language. He must have heard me talking to the ox, and this is why he threatened to send it to the butcher. But he did nothing to me, and has in fact repaid intrigue with kindness.'

She brayed: 'Thank you, master.' Timur laughed at the secret which he had, but his wife was furious.

'I think that you know something about the ways these animals are talking,' she said.

'Who ever heard of an animal talking?' asked Timur.

When they got home, he bedded the ox down in fresh straw which they had bought, and it said: 'You are harassed by your wife, and your secret will at this rate soon be out. If you only realized it, poor man, you could make her behave and keep yourself safe merely by threatening her with a beating with a stick no thicker than your little finger.'

'Thus it is', thought Timur, 'that this ox, whom I threatened with the slaughterhouse, thinks of my welfare.'

So he went to his wife and took up a small stick, and said: 'Will you behave? Will you stop asking me questions even when I so much as laugh?'

She was thoroughly alarmed, for he had never spoken like that to her before. And he never had to tell her, and thus was preserved from the awful fate which awaits those who give away secrets to others who are not ready to receive them.

ров

Timur Agha and the Speech of Animals

Timur Agha has, in his folklore, the reputation of being able to perceive significance in things which are apparently unimportant.

This story is said to confer 'baraka' — blessings — upon the teller and the hearer, and hence is popular in the Balkans and the Near East. Many Sufic stories are disguised as fairy tales.

This story is attributed (in an earlier form) to Abu-Ishak Chishti, tenth-century leader of the 'Singing Dervishes'.

The Indian Bird

A MERCHANT kept a bird in a cage. He was going to India, the land from which the bird came, and asked it whether he could bring anything back for it. The bird asked for its freedom, but was refused. So he asked the merchant to visit a jungle in India and announce his captivity to the free birds who were there.

The merchant did so, and no sooner had he spoken when a wild bird, just like his own, fell senseless out of a tree on to the ground.

The merchant thought that this must be a relative of his own bird, and felt sad that he should have caused this death.

When he got home, the bird asked him whether he had brought good news from India.

'No,' said the merchant, 'I fear that my news is bad. One of your relations collapsed and fell at my feet when I mentioned your captivity.'

As soon as these words were spoken the merchant's bird collapsed and fell to the bottom of the cage.

'The news of his kinsman's death has killed him, too,' thought the merchant. Sorrowfully he picked up the bird and put it on the window-sill. At once the bird revived and flew to a near-by tree.

'Now you know', the bird said, 'that what you thought was disaster was in fact good news for me. And how the message, the suggestion of how to behave in order to free myself, was transmitted to me through you, my captor.' And he flew away, free at last.

୨୨

Rumi's fable is one of many which stress for the Sufi Seeker the great importance played in Sufism by indirect learning.

Imitators and systems styled to accord with conventional thinking, in East and West alike, generally prefer to emphasize 'system' and 'programme', rather than the totality of experience which takes place in a Sufi school.

When Death Came to Baghdad

THE disciple of a Sufi of Baghdad was sitting in the corner of an inn one day when he heard two figures talking. From what they said he realized that one of them was the Angel of Death.

'I have several calls to make in this city during the next three weeks,' the Angel was saying to his companion.

Terrified, the disciple concealed himself until the two had left. Then, applying his intelligence to the problem of how to cheat a possible call from death, he decided that if he kept away from Baghdad he should not be touched. From this reasoning it was but a short step to hiring the fastest horse available and spurring it night and day towards the distant town of Samarkand.

Meanwhile Death met the Sufi teacher and they talked about various people. 'And where is your disciple so-and-so?' asked Death.

'He should be somewhere in this city, spending his time in contemplation, perhaps in a caravanserai,' said the teacher.

'Surprising,' said the Angel; 'because he is on my list. Yes, here it is: I have to collect him in four weeks' time at Samarkand, of all places.'

೫

This treatment of the Story of Death is taken from Hikayat-i-Naqshia ('Tales formed according to a design').

The author of this story, which is a very favourite folklore story in the Middle East, was the great Sufi Fudail ibn Ayad, a former highwayman, who died in the early part of the ninth century.

According to Sufi tradition, confirmed by historical material, Haroun el-Raschid the Caliph of Baghdad tried to concentrate 'all knowledge' at his court. Various Sufis lived under his patronage, but none allowed this all-powerful monarch to enlist him in his service.

Sufi historians relate how Haroun and his Vizier visited Mecca to see Fudail, who said: 'Commander of the Faithful! I fear that your comely face may fall into hell-fire!'

Haroun asked the sage: 'Have you ever known anyone with greater detachment than you have?'

Fudail said: 'Yes, you have greater detachment than I. I can detach from the environment of the customary world; but you have detached yourself from something much greater, from that which is everlasting!'

Fudail told the Caliph that power over oneself was better than a thousand years of power over others.

The Grammarian and the Dervish

ONE dark night a dervish was passing a dry well when he heard a cry for help from below. 'What is the matter?' he called down.

'I am a grammarian, and I have unfortunately fallen, due to my ignorance of the path, into this deep well, in which I am now all but immobilized,' responded the other.

'Hold, friend, and I'll fetch a ladder and rope,' said the dervish.

'One moment, please!' said the grammarian. 'Your grammar and diction are faulty; be good enough to amend them.'

'If that is so much more important than the essentials,' shouted the dervish, '*you* had best stay where you are until *I* have learned to speak properly.'

And he went his way.

This tale was related by Jalaludin Rumi and is recorded in Aflaki's *Acts of the Adepts*. Published in England in 1965, under the title of *Legends of the Sufis*, this account of the Mevlevis and their supposed doings was written in the fourteenth century.

Some of the stories are mere wonder-tales, but others are historical: and some are of the strange type known by the Sufis as 'illustrative history': that is to say, a series of events are concocted to point a meaning connected with psychological processes.

For this reason such tales have been called 'The Artistry of the Dervish scientists'.

The Dervish and the Princess

A KING's daughter was as fair as the moon, and admired by all.

A dervish saw her one day, as he was about to eat a piece of bread. The morsel fell to the ground, for he was so deeply moved that he could not hold it.

As she passed by she smiled upon him. This action sent him into convulsions, his bread in the dust, his senses half bereft. In a state of ecstasy he remained thus for seven years. The dervish spent all that time in the street, where dogs slept.

He was a nuisance to the princess, and her attendants decided to kill him.

But she called him to her and said: 'There can be no union between you and me. And my slaves intend to kill you; therefore disappear.'

The miserable man answered: 'Since I first saw you, life is nothing to me. They will kill me without cause. But please answer me one question, since you are to be the cause of my death. Why did you smile at all?'

'Foolish man!' said the princess. 'When I saw what a fool you were making yourself, I smiled in pity, not for any other reason.'

And she disappeared from his sight.

In his *Parliament of the Birds*, Attar speaks of the misunderstanding of subjective emotions which causes men to believe that certain experiences ('the smile of the princess') are special gifts ('admiration') whereas they may be the very reverse ('pity').

Many have been misled, because this kind of literature has its own conventions, into believing that Sufi classical writings are other than technical descriptions of psychological states.

194

The Increasing of Necessity

THE tyrannical ruler of Turkestan was listening to the tales of a dervish one evening, when he bethought himself of asking about Khidr.

'Khidr', said the dervish, 'comes in response to need. Seize his coat when he appears, and all-knowledge is yours.'

'Can this happen to anyone?' asked the king.

'Anyone capable,' said the dervish.

'Who more "capable" than I?' thought the king, and he published a proclamation:

'He who presents to me the Invisible Khidr, the Great Protector of Men, him shall I enrich.'

A poor old man by the name of Bakhtiar Baba, hearing this cried by the heralds, formed an idea. He said to his wife:

'I have a plan. We shall soon be rich, but a little later I shall have to die. But this does not matter, for our riches will leave you well provided for.'

Then Bakhtiar went before the king and told him that he would find Khidr within forty days, if the king would give him a thousand pieces of gold. 'If you find Khidr,' said the king, 'you shall have ten times this thousand pieces of gold. If you do not, you will die, executed at this very spot as a warning to those who trifle with kings.'

Bakhtiar accepted the conditions. He returned home and gave the money to his wife, as a provision for the rest of her life. The rest of the forty days he spent in contemplation, preparing himself for the other life.

On the fortieth day he went before the king. 'Your Majesty,' he said, 'your greed caused you to think that money would produce Khidr. But Khidr, as it is related, does not appear in response to something given from a position of greed.'

The king was furious. 'Wretch, you have forfeited your life: who are you to trifle with the aspirations of a king?'

Bakhtiar said: 'Legend has it that any man may meet Khidr, but the meeting will be fruitful only in so far as that man's intentions are correct. Khidr, they say, would visit you to the extent and for the period that you were worth his while being visited. This is something over which neither you nor I has any control.'

'Enough of this wrangling,' said the king, 'for it will not prolong your life. It only remains to ask the ministers assembled here for their advice upon the best way to put you to death.'

He turned to the First Wazir and said: 'How shall this man die?'

The First Wazir said: 'Roast him alive, as a warning.'

The Second Wazir, speaking in order of precedence, said: 'Dismember him, limb from limb.'

The Third Wazir said: 'Provide him with the necessities of life, instead of forcing him to cheat in order to provide for his family.'

While this discussion was going on, an ancient sage had walked into the assembly hall. As soon as the Third Wazir had spoken, he said: 'Every man opines in accordance with his permanent hidden prejudices.'

'What do you mean?' asked the king.

'I mean that the First Wazir was originally a baker, so he speaks in terms of roasting. The Second Wazir used to be a butcher, so he talks about dismemberment. The Third Wazir, having made a study of statecraft, sees the origin of the matter we are discussing.

'Note two things. First, that Khidr appears and serves each man in accordance with that man's ability to profit by his coming. Second, that this man Bakhtiar, whom I name Baba in token of his sacrifices, was driven by despair to do what he did. He increased his necessity and accordingly he made me appear to you.'

As they watched, the ancient sage melted before their eyes. Trying to do what Khidr directed, the king gave a permanent allowance to Bakhtiar. The First Two Wazirs were dismissed, and the thousand pieces of gold were returned to the royal treasury by the grateful Bakhtiar Baba and his wife.

How the king was able to see Khidr again, and what transpired between them is in the story of the story of the story of the Unseen World.

 හං

Bakhtiar Baba is said to have been a Sufi sage who lived a humble and unremarkable life in Khorasan until the events described above.

This tale, attributed also to many other Sufi sheikhs, illustrates the concept of the entwining of human aspiration with another range of being. Khidr is the link between these two spheres.

The title is taken from Jalaludin Rumi's famous poem:

New organs of perception come into being as a result of necessity.
Therefore, O man, increase your necessity, so that you may increase your perception.

This version comes from the lips of a dervish master of Afghanistan.

The Man Who Looked Only at the Obvious

A SEEKER after Truth, after many vicissitudes, at last found an enlightened man, endowed with perception of things not available to all.

The Seeker said to him: 'Allow me to follow you, so that I may learn by observing what you have acquired.'

The Wise One answered: 'You will not be able to endure it, for you will not have the patience to stay in contact, diligently, with the pattern of events. You will try to act in obvious ways instead of learning.'

The Seeker promised that he would try to exercise patience, and learn from what happened, without acting in accordance with existing prejudice.

'Then I make one condition,' said the Wise One, 'and that is that you must ask nothing about any event, until such time as myself give you an answer.'

The Seeker promised eagerly enough, and they set off on a journey.

Scarcely had they boarded the boat which was to take them across a wide river, when the Wise One secretly made a hole in the bottom, causing a leak, and seemingly repaying the ferryman's help with destructive action.

The Seeker could not contain himself. 'People may be drowned, the boat will be sunk and lost! Is this the action of a good man?'

'I told you, did I not,' remarked the Wise One mildly, 'that you would not be able to avoid jumping to conclusions?'

'I had already forgotten the condition,' said the Seeker. And he asked to be forgiven for the slip. But he was very puzzled.

Their journey continued until they came to a country where they were treated well, welcomed by the king, and asked to go hunting with him. The small son of the king was mounted in front of the Wise One. As soon as he and the Seeker were separated by a thicket from the rest of the hunt, the Wise One said: 'Quick, follow me as fast as you can.' He twisted the ankle of the young Prince, deposited the child in the thicket, and rode his horse as fast as he could beyond the boundaries of the Kingdom.

The Seeker was overwhelmed with shock and the guilt of having been a party to this crime. Wringing his hands, he exclaimed: 'A king befriended us, trusted us with his son and heir, and we dealt abominably with him! What kind of conduct is this? Unworthy of the meanest of men!'

The Wise One simply turned to the Seeker and said to him: 'Friend, I am carrying on with what I have to do. You are an observer and few people even reach this position of observer. Having reached it, it seems to me that you cannot make any use of it, for you are judging from your fixed position of prejudice. I again remind you of your promise.'

'I recognize that I would not be here but for my promise, and that that promise is binding upon me,' said the Seeker. 'Please, therefore, forgive me once again; I find the habit of working from assumptions hard to break. If I should question you but once again, dismiss me from your company.'

They journeyed on.

Reaching a large and prosperous city, the travellers asked for a little food, but nobody would give them even a scrap. Charity was unknown here, and the sacred obligations of guesthood had been forgotten. On the contrary, wild dogs were set upon them.

As they reached the outskirts of the city, hungry, faint and thirsty, the Seeker's companion said: 'Stop awhile here by this ruined wall, for we must repair it.'

For some hours they laboured, mixing mud, straw and water, until the wall was restored.

The Seeker was so exhausted that his discipline deserted him, and he said: 'We will not be paid for this. We have twice repaid good with evil. Now we repay evil with good. I am at the end of my tether, and cannot go further.'

'Have no more fear,' said the Wise One, 'and remember that you said that if you questioned me just once more I should dismiss you. Our ways part here, for I have much to do.

'Before I leave you, I will explain the meaning of some of my actions, so that perhaps one day you will again be able to go on a journey such as this.

'The boat I damaged sank and was thus spared confiscation by a tyrant who was seizing all boats for a war. The boy whose ankle I twisted cannot now grow up to be a usurper, or even inherit the Kingdom, because the Law says that only the physically complete may lead the nation. In this city of hatred are two young orphans. When they grow up, the wall will again crumble and reveal the hoard concealed within it, which is their patrimony. They will be strong enough to take possession of it and reform the whole city, for this is their destiny.

'Go now, in peace. You are dismissed.'

ೞ

This tale was told and retold in the Middle Ages as a Christian story by the monks who used the *Gesta Romanorum* as their source of uplifting 'applications'.

It is also said to be the original of Parnell's *Hermit*. Pope said that its original was Spanish; and, although it has been suspected of being an oriental tale, for long nobody in the West seems to have connected it with the Sufis; or to have noted that its first appearance was in the Koran, Chap. 18, *The Cave*.

It is related in the above form by Jan-Fishan Khan.

How Knowledge was Earned

ᴏɴᴄᴇ upon a time there was a man who decided that he needed knowledge. He set off to look for it, bending his steps towards the house of a learned man.

When he got there he said: 'Sufi, you are a wise man! Let me have a portion of your knowledge, so that I may grow it and become worthwhile, for I feel that I am nothing.'

The Sufi said: 'I can give you knowledge in exchange for something which I myself need. Go and bring me a small carpet, for I have to give it to someone who will then be able to further our holy work.'

So the man set off. He arrived at a carpet-shop and said to the owner: 'Give me a carpet, just a small one, for I have to give it to a Sufi, who will give me knowledge. He needs the carpet to give to someone who will be able to further our holy work.'

The carpet dealer said: 'That is a description of your stage, and the work of the Sufi, and the needs of the man who is to use the carpet. What about me? I need thread for weaving carpets. Bring me some and I will help you.'

So the man went off, looking for someone who could let him have thread. When he arrived at the hut of a spinner-woman, he said to her: 'Spinner-woman, give me thread. I have to have it for the carpet-man, who will give me a carpet which I will give to a Sufi, who will give it to a man who has to do our holy work. In exchange I will get knowledge, which I want.'

The woman immediately answered: 'You need thread, what about me? Away with this talk about you, and your Sufi and your carpet-man and the man who has to have the carpet. What about me? I need goat-hair to make thread. Get me some and you can have your thread.'

So the man went off, until he came to a goat-herd, and he told him his needs. The goat-herd said: 'What about me? You need goat-hair to buy knowledge, I need goats to provide the hair. Get me a goat and I shall help you.'

So the man went off, looking for someone who sold goats. When he found such a man he told him his difficulties, and the man said: 'What do I know about knowledge, or thread or carpets? All I know is that everyone seems to be looking after his own interests. Let us instead talk about my needs, and if you can satisfy them, then we will talk about goats, and you can think about knowledge all you wish.'

'What are you needs?' asked the man.

'I need a pen to keep my goats in at night, because they are straying all over the place. Get me one and then talk about your having a goat or two.'

So the man went off to look for a pen. His inquiries led him to a carpenter, who said: 'Yes, I can make a pen for the man who needs one. As for the rest, you could have spared me the details, for I am just not interested in carpets or knowledge and the like. But I have a desire, and it is in your interests to help me gain it, otherwise I need not help you with your pen.'

'And what is that desire?' asked the man.

'I want to get married and nobody will marry me, it seems. See whether you can arrange a wife for me, and then we will talk about your problems.'

So the man went off, and after making exhaustive inquiries he found a woman who said: 'I know a young woman who has no other desire than to marry just such a carpenter as you describe. In fact she has been thinking about him all her life. It must be some sort of miracle that he does exist and that she can hear of him through you and me. But what about me? Everyone wants what he wants, and people seem to need things, or want things, or imagine that they need help, or really want help, but nobody has yet said anything about *my* needs.'

'And what are your needs?' asked the man.

'I want only one thing,' said the woman, 'and I have wanted it all my life. Help me to get it, and you can have anything I have.

The thing that I want, as I have experienced everything else, is — knowledge.'

'But we cannot have knowledge without a carpet,' said the man.

'I do not know what knowledge is, but I am sure that it is not a carpet,' said the woman.

'No', said the man, seeing that he had to be patient, 'but with the girl for the carpenter we can get the pen for the goats. With the pen for the goats we can get the goat-hair for the spinner. With the goat-hair we can get the thread. With the thread we can get the carpet. With the carpet we can get the knowledge.'

'It sound preposterous to me,' said the woman, 'and I for one am not going to go to those lengths.'

In spite of his entreaties, she sent him away.

These difficulties and the confusion which they caused him first made him almost despair of the human race. He wondered whether he could use knowledge when he got it, and he wondered why all those people were only thinking of their own interests. And slowly he began to think only of the carpet.

One day this man was wandering through the streets of a market-town, muttering to himself.

A certain merchant heard him, and drew near to catch his words. The man was saying: 'A carpet is needed to give to a man so that he may be able to do this holy work of ours.'

The merchant realized that there was something exceptional about the wanderer, and addressed him:

'Wandering dervish, I do not understand your chant, but I have deep respect for one such as you, who has embarked upon the Path of Truth. Please help me, if you will, for I know that the people of the Sufi way have a special function in society.'

The wanderer looked up and saw the distress on the merchant's face and said to him: 'I am suffering and I have suffered. You are undoubtedly in trouble, but I have nothing. I cannot even get a piece of thread when I want it. But ask me and I will do anything that I can.'

'Know, fortunate man!' said the merchant, 'that I have an only and beautiful daughter. She is suffering from an illness which has caused her to languish. Come to her and perhaps you will be able to effect a cure.'

Such was the man's distress and so high were his hopes that the wanderer followed him to the girl's bedside.

As soon as she saw him, she said: 'I do not know who you are, but I feel you may be able to help me. In any case there is nobody else. I am in love with such-and-such a carpenter.' And she named the man whom the traveller had asked to make the pen for the goats.

'Your daughter wants to marry a certain respectable carpenter whom I know,' he told the merchant. The merchant was overjoyed, for he had thought that the girl's talk about the carpenter had been the symptom, not the cause, of her disease. He had, in fact, thought her mad.

The traveller went to the carpenter, who built the pen for the goats. The goat-seller presented him with some fine animals; he took them to the goat-herd, who gave him goat-hair, which he took to the spinner, who gave him thread. Then he took the thread to the carpet-seller, who gave him a small carpet.

This carpet he carried back to the Sufi. When he arrived at the house of the wise man, the latter said to him: 'Now I can give you knowledge; for you could not have brought this carpet unless you had worked for the carpet, and not for yourself.'

соч

The 'hidden dimension' in life, by knowledge of which a Sufi master induces his pupil to undergo development in spite of his desires — sometimes by harnessing them — is well portrayed in this tale.

It is chosen from the oral traditions of the dervishes of Badakhshan, and in this fairy-tale form carries the authority of Khwaja Mohamed Baba Samasi. He was Grand Master of the Order of the Masters, third in line before Bahaudin Naqshband, and died in 1354.

The Lamp Shop

ONE dark night two men met on a lonely road.

'I am looking for a shop near here, which is called The Lamp Shop,' said the first man.

'I happen to live near here, and I can direct you to it,' said the second man.

'I should be able to find it by myself. I have been given the directions, and I have written them down,' said the first man.

'Then why are you talking to me about it?'

'Just talking.'

'So you want company, not directions?'

'Yes, I suppose that that is what it is.'

'But it would be easier for you to take further directions from a local resident, having got so far: especially because from here onwards it is difficult.'

'I trust what I have already been told, which has brought me thus far. I cannot be sure that I can trust anything or anyone else.'

'So, although you once trusted the original informant, you have not been taught a means of knowing whom you can trust?'

'That is so.'

'Have you any other aim?'

'No, just to find the Lamp Shop.'

'May I ask why you seek a lamp shop?'

'Because I have been told on the highest authority that that is where they supply certain devices which enable a person to read in the dark.'

'You are correct, but there is a prerequisite, and also a piece of information. I wonder whether you have given them any thought.'

'What are they?'

'The prerequisite to reading by means of a lamp is *that you can already read.*'

'You cannot prove that!'

'Certainly not on a dark night like this.'

'What is the "Piece of information"?'

'The piece of information is that the Lamp Shop is still where it always was, but that the lamps themselves have been moved somewhere else.'

'I do not know what a "Lamp" is, but it seems obvious to me that the Lamp Shop is the place to locate such a device. That is, after all, why it is called a Lamp Shop.'

'But a "Lamp Shop" may have two different meanings, each opposed to the other. The meanings are: "A place where lamps may be obtained", and "A place where lamps were once obtained but which now has none".'

'You cannot prove that!'

'You would seem like an idiot to many people.'

'But there are many people who would call *you* an idiot. Yet perhaps you are not. You probably have an ulterior motive, sending me off to some place where lamps are sold by a friend of yours. Or perhaps you do not want me to have a lamp at all.'

'I am worse than you think. Instead of promising you "Lamp Shops" and allowing you to assume that you will find the answer to your problems there, I would first of all find out if you could read at all. I would find out if you were near such a shop. Or whether a lamp might be obtained for you in some other way.'

The two men looked at each other, sadly, for a moment. Then each went his way.

ಬಿ

Shaikh-Pir Shattari, the author of this story, died in India in 1632. His shrine is at Meerut.

He is credited with maintaining a telepathic contact with 'past, present and future' teachers, and giving them the means to project their message through his speciality of stories based upon the everyday life of the community.

The Chariot

THERE are three sciences in the study of man. The first is the Science of ordinary knowledge; the second is the Science of un-usual inner states, often called ecstasy. The third, which is the important one, is the Science of True Reality: of what lies beyond these two.

Only the real inner knowledge carries with it the knowledge of the Science of True Reality. The other two are the reflections, in their own form, of the third. They are almost useless without it.

Picture a charioteer. He is seated in a vehicle, propelled by a horse, guided by himself. Intellect is the 'vehicle', the outward form within which we state where we think we are and what we have to do. The vehicle enables the horse and man to operate. This is what we tall *tashkil*, outward shape or formulation. The horse, which is the motive power, is the energy which is called 'a state of emotion' or other force. This is needed to propel the chariot. The man, in our illustration, is that which perceives, in a manner superior to the others, the purpose and possibilities of the situation, and who makes it possible for the chariot to move towards and to gain its objective.

One of the three, on its own, will be able to fulfil functions, true enough. But the combined function which we call the movement of the chariot cannot take place unless all three are connected in the Right Way.

Only the 'man', the real Self, knows the relationship of the three elements, and their need of one another.

Among the Sufis, the Great Work is the knowledge of combining the three elements. Too many men, too unsuitable a horse, too light or too heavy a chariot—and the result will not take place.

಄

The Chariot

This fragment is recorded in a dervish notebook in Persian, and various forms of the story are found in Sufi schools as far apart as Damascus and Delhi.

The Lame Man and the Blind Man

～～～～～～～～～～～～～～～～～～～～～～～～～～

A LAME man walked into a Serai ('Inn') one day, and sat down beside a figure already seated there. 'I shall never be able to reach the Sultan's banquet', he sighed, 'because, due to my infirmity, I am unable to move fast enough.'

The other man raised his head. 'I, too, have been invited,' he said, 'but my plight is worse than yours. I am blind, and cannot see the road, although I have also been invited.'

A third man who heard them talking said: 'But, if you only realized it, you two have between you the means to reach your destination. The blind man can walk, with the lame one on his back. You can use the feet of the blind man and the eyes of the lame to direct you.'

Thus the two were able to reach the end of the road, where the feast awaited them.

But on their way, they stopped to rest at another Serai. They explained their condition to two other men who were sitting disconsolately there. Of these two, one was deaf and the other dumb. They had both been invited to the feast. The dumb one had heard but was unable to explain to his friend the deaf man. The deaf man could talk but had nothing to say.

Neither of them arrived at the feast; for this time there was no third man to explain to them that there was a difficulty, let alone how they might resolve it.

～～

It is related that the great Abdul-Qadir left a patched Sufi cloak to be presented to a successor to his mantle who was to be born nearly six hundred years after his death.

In 1563 Sayed Sikandar Shah, Qadiri, having inherited this trust, located and invested with the mantle the Sheikh Ahmed Faruqi of Sirhind.

This Naqshbandi teacher had already been initiated into sixteen Dervish Orders by his father, who had sought and reconstituted the scattered lore of Sufism in extensive and perilous journeys.

It is believed that Sirhind was the place designated for the appearance of the Great Teacher, and a succession of saints had awaited his manifestation for generations.

As a consequence of the appearance of Faruqi and his acceptance by the chiefs of all the Orders of the time, the Naqshbandis now initiate disciples into all of the four major streams of Sufism: the Chishti, Qadiri, Suhrawardi and Naqshbandi Ways.

'The Lame Man and the Blind Man' is ascribed to Sheikh Ahmed Faruqi, who died in 1615. It is supposed to be read only after receiving definite instructions to do so: or by those who have already studied Hakim Sanai's 'Blind Ones and the Matter of the Elephant'.

The Servants and the House

AT ONE time there was a wise and kindly man, who owned a large house. In the course of his life he often had to go away for long periods. When he did this, he left the house in the charge of his servants.

One of the characteristics of these people was that they were very forgetful. They forgot, from time to time, why they were in the house; so they carried out their tasks repetitiously. At other times they thought that they should be doing things in a different way from the way in which their duties had been assigned to them. This was because they had lost track of their functions.

Once, when the master was away for a long time, a new generation of servants arose, who thought that they actually owned the house. Since they were limited by their immediate world, however, they thought that they were in a paradoxical situation. For instance, sometimes they wanted to sell the house, and could find no buyers, because they did not know how to go about it. At other times people came inquiring about buying the house and asking to see the title-deeds, but since they did not know anything about deeds the servants thought that these people were mad and not genuine buyers at all.

Paradox was also evidenced by the fact that supplies for the house kept 'mysteriously' appearing, and this provision did not fit in with the assumption that the inmates were responsible for the whole house.

Instructions for running the house had been left, for purposes of refreshing the memory, in the master's apartments. But after the first generation, so sacrosanct had these apartments become that nobody was allowed to enter them, and they became considered to be an impenetrable mystery. Some, indeed, held that there was no such apartment at all, although they could see its doors. These doors, however, they explained as something else: a part of the decoration of the walls.

Such was the condition of the staff of a house, which neither took over the house nor stayed faithful to their original commitment.

∞

Tradition states that this tale was much used by the Sufi martyr el-Hallaj, who was executed in 922 for allegedly saying: 'I am the Truth.'

Hallaj left behind a remarkable collection of mystical poetry. At great risk to themselves, many Sufis during the last thousand years have steadfastly maintained that Hallaj was a high illuminate.

The Generous Man

THERE was a rich and generous man of Bokhara. Because he had such high rank in the invisible hierarchy, he was known as the President of the World. He made one condition about his bounty. Every day he gave gold to one category of people — the sick, widows, and so on. But nothing was to be given to anyone who opened his mouth.

Not all could keep silent.

One day it was the turn of lawyers to receive their share of the bounty. One of them could not restrain himself and made the most complete appeal possible.

Nothing was given to him.

This was not the end, however, of his efforts. The following day invalids were being helped, so he pretended that his limbs had been broken.

But the President knew him, and he obtained nothing.

The very next day he posed in another guise, covering his face, with the people of another category. He was again recognized and sent away.

Again and again he tried, even disguising himself as a woman: again without result.

Finally this lawyer found an undertaker and told him to wrap him in a shroud. 'When the President passes by he will perhaps assume that this is a corpse. He may throw down some money towards my burial — and I will give you a share of it.'

This was done. A gold piece from the hand of the President fell upon the shroud. The beggar seized it, out of fear that the undertaker would get it first. Then he spoke to the benefactor: 'You denied me your bounty. Note how I have gained it!'

'Nothing can you have from me', replied the generous man, 'until you die. This is the meaning of the cryptic phrase "man must die before he dies". The gift comes after "death" and not before. And this "death", even, is not possible without help.'

၇၈၁

This tale, from the Fourth Book of the *Mathnavi* of Rumi, explains itself.

Dervishes use it to emphasize that, while certain endowments can be 'snatched' by the wily, the capacity ('gold') which is willingly extracted from a teacher like the Generous Man of Bokhara has a power beyond that of its appearance. This is the elusive quality of Baraka.

The Host and the Guests

THE teacher is like the host in his house. His guests are those who are trying to study the Way. These are people who have never been in a house before, and they only have vague ideas as to what a house may be like. It exists, nevertheless.

When the guests enter the house and see the place set aside for sitting in, they ask: 'What is this?' They are told: 'This is a place where we sit.' So they sit down on chairs, only dimly conscious of the function of the chair.

The host entertains them, but they continue to ask questions, some irrelevant. Like a good host, he does not blame them for this. They want to know, for instance, where and when they are going to eat. They do not know that nobody is alone, and that at that very moment there are other people who are cooking the food, and that there is another room in which they will sit down and have a meal. Because they cannot see the meal, or its preparation, they are confused, perhaps doubtful, sometimes ill at ease.

The good host, knowing the problems of the guests, has to put them at their ease, so that they will be able to enjoy the food when it comes. At the outset they are in no state to approach the food.

Some of the guests are quicker to understand and relate one thing about the house to another thing. These are the ones who can communicate to their slower friends. The host, meanwhile, gives each guest an answer in accordance with his capacity to perceive the unity and function of the house.

It is not enough for a house to exist, for it to be made ready to receive guests, for the host to be present. Someone must actively exercise the function of host, in order that the strangers who are the guests, and for whom the host has responsibility, may become accustomed to the house. At the beginning, many of them are not aware that they are guests, or rather exactly what guesthood means: what they can bring to it, what it can give them.

The experienced guest, who has learned about houses and hospitality, is at length at ease in his guesthood, and he is then in a position to understand more about houses and about many facets of living in them. While he is still trying to understand what a house is, or trying to remember rules of etiquette, his attention is too much taken up by these factors to be able to observe, say, the beauty, value or function of the furniture.

∞

This venerated parable, quoted from the teachings of the fourteenth-century Nizamudin Awlia, is supposed to hold good on several levels. It refers to the ordering of the various functions of the mind, in order that a certain higher perception may be able to develop.

The story is also intended to indicate, in a manner which can easily be held in the mind, the necessities of a Sufi group, and the inter-relation between the various members, and how each can complement the others.

Much emphasis is placed by dervishes in the need for a certain arrangement of factors before the individual can benefit from the efforts of the group.

This is one of the Sufi tales which carry an embargo. It may not be studied in isolation, and wherever it is written down, the student must read the following story immediately after this one.

It does not appear in any classic, but may be found in those collections of notes which dervishes carry with them, and refer to from time to time, as part of a planned course of study.

This version is taken from a manuscript which states that it was given out by Master Amir-Sayed Kulal Sokhari, who died in 1371.

The King's Son

ᘛᘚᘛᘚᘛᘚᘛᘚ ᘛᘚᘛᘚᘛᘚᘛᘚᘛᘚᘛᘚᘛᘚᘛᘚᘛᘚ ᘛᘚᘛᘚᘛᘚᘛᘚᘛᘚᘛᘚᘛᘚᘛᘚᘛᘚ ᘛᘚᘛᘚ

ONCE in a country where all men were like kings, there lived a family, who were in every way content, and whose surroundings were such that the human tongue cannot describe them in terms of anything which is known to man today. This country of Sharq seemed satisfactory to the young prince Dhat: until one day his parents told him: 'Dearest son of ours, it is the necessary custom of our land for each royal prince, when he attains a certain age, to go forth on a trial. This is in order to fit himself for kingship and so that both in repute and in fact he should have achieved — by watchfulness and effort — a degree of manliness not to be attained in any other way. Thus it has been ordained from the beginning, and thus it will be until the end.'

Prince Dhat therefore prepared himself for his journey, and his family provided him with such sustenance they could: a special food which would nourish him during an exile, but which was of small compass though of illimitable quantity.

They also gave him certain other resources, which it is not possible to mention, to guard him, if they were properly used.

He had to travel to a certain country, called Misr, and he had to go in disguise. He was therefore given guides for the journey, and clothes befitting his new condition: clothes which scarcely resembled one royal-born. His task was to bring back from Misr a certain Jewel, which was guarded by a fearsome monster.

When his guides departed, Dhat was alone, but before long he came across someone else who was on a similar mission, and together they were able to keep alive the memory of their sublime origins. But, because of the air and the food of the country, a kind of sleep soon descended upon the pair, and Dhat forgot his mission.

For years he lived in Misr, earning his keep and following a humble vocation, seemingly unaware of what he should be doing.

By a means which was familiar to them but unknown to other people, the inhabitants of Sharq came to know of the dire situation of Dhat, and they worked together in such a way as they could, to help to release him and to enable him to persevere with his mission. A message was sent by a strange means to the princeling, saying: 'Awake! For you are the son of a king, sent on a special undertaking, and to us you must return.'

This message awoke the prince, who found his way to the monster, and by the use of special sounds, caused it to fall into a sleep; and he seized the priceless gem which it had been guarding.

Now Dhat followed the sounds of the message which had woken him, changed his garb for that of his own land, and retraced his steps, guided by the Sound, to the country of Sharq.

In a surprisingly short time, Dhat again beheld his ancient robes, and the country of his fathers, and reached his home. This time, however, through his experiences, he was able to see that it was somewhere of greater splendour than ever before, a safety to him; and he realized that it was the place commemorated vaguely by the people of Misr as Salamat: which they took to be the word for Submission, but which he now realized meant — peace.

※

Very much the same theme is found in the Hymn of the Soul in the New Testament Apocrypha. The philosopher Ibn-Sina (died 1038), who is known as Avicenna in the West, has dealt with the same material in his allegory of the Soul's Exile, or Poem of the Soul.

This version appears in a wandering dervish's transcription from a recital supposedly given by Amir Sultan, Sheikh of Bokhara, who taught in Istanbul and died in 1429.

Appendix

ϱϗ

Authors and teachers referred to in this book, in chronological order

The dates are expressed in terms of the Christian era, and the entries refer to the date of death.

7th century

634   Abu-Bakr el-Saddiq, Companion of the Prophet and First Caliph.

657   Hadrat Uwais el-Qarni, Guide of the Uwaisi Sufis, contemporary of Mohammed.

661   Hadrat Ali, son of Abu-Talib, son-in-law, Companion and Fourth Caliph of Mohammed.

680   Sayed Hussein, son of Hadrat Ali, martyred.

8th century

728   Hasan of Basra, born Medina, orator and Sufi Ancient.

790   Jabir, son of el-Hayyan, disciple of Jafar, 'Geber the Alchemist' in European literature.

9th century

803   Fudail, son of Ayad, 'The Highwayman', died Mecca. Taught Caliph Haroun el-Raschid.

828   Abu el-Atahiyya, founder of the 'Revellers', poet.

860   Dhun-Nun the Egyptian, 'Lord of the Fish', hieroglyphicist.

875   Bayazid (Abu-Yazid) of Bistam, 'Leader of the Learned'.

885   Abu-Ali of Sind, teacher of Bayazid, lacked formal knowledge of Islam, but communicated Sufi experiences.

10th century

922   Mansur el-Hallaj, 'The Wool-Carder' (executed for apostasy).

934   Abu-Ali Mohammed, son of el-Qasim el-Rudbari.

c.965   El-Mutanabbi, classical Arabic poet.

     Abu-Ishak Chishti, of Turkestan.

APPENDIX

11th century

1038   Ibn-Sina ('Avicenna' to the West), philosopher.

1072   Ali el-Hujwiri, saint and author of *The Revelation of the Veiled*.

1078   Khaja ('Master') Ali Farmadhi, of the Naqshbandi Chain of Succession.

1089   Khaja Abdullah Ansar, classical poet and mystic, buried at Gazargah.

12th century

1111   Imam el-Ghazali of Persia (*The Proof of Islam*), teacher and author of classics in Arabic and Persian.

1140   Yusuf Hamadani.

1150   Hakim Sanai of Ghazna, Afghanistan, author of many classics, including *The Walled Garden of Truth* (1130).

1166   Hadrat Abdul-Qadir of Gilan, founder of the Qadiri Order.

1174   Ahmed el-Rifai, founder of the Rifai ('Howling') Dervishes.

3th century

1221   Najmudin Kubra ('The Greatest Scourge'—in debate), fell in battle.

1230   Sheikh Faridudin Attar, inspirer of Rumi, author of Sufi classics.

1234   Sheikh Shahabudin Omar Suhrawardi, disciple of Abdul-Qadir of Gilan, author of the *Gifts of Deep Knowledge*.

1273   Maulana Jalaludin 'Rumi' of Balkh (Afghanistan). Taught in Rum (Iconium). Author of *Mathnavi*, etc.

1276   Sheikh Ahmed el-Bedavi, founded Bedavi Order in Egypt.

1294   Majnun Qalandar ('The Mad Wanderer'), said to have taught only by telepathy.
       Yusuf Qalandar of Andalusia, mentor of the 'Wandering' Dervishes.

14th century

1306   Khaja Ali Ramitani of Turkestan, teacher of the Khajagan ('Masters').

1311   Timur Agha of Turkey.

1325   Nizamudin Awlia, great saint of India.

1354   Khaja Mohamed Baba Samasi, teacher of the Khajagan.

1371 Khaja Amir-Sayed Kulal Sokhari, teacher of the Naqshbandi Chain.

1382 Bakhtiar Baba.

c.1389 Maulana Hadrat Bahaudin Naqshband, 'The Shah', teacher of the Naqshbandi/Khajagan.

1397 Hadrat Omar Khilwati, founder of the Khilwati ('Recluse') Order.

15th century

1429 Amir Sultan, Sheikh of Bokhara.

1492 Hakim Nurudin Abdur-Rahman Jami, classical Persian author.

16th century

1563 Shah Mohammed Gwath Shattari, founded Shattari ('Rapid') Order.

1563 Sikander Shah, Qadiri.

1575 Sheikh Hamza Malamati Maqtul (executed).

17th century

1605 Amil-Baba ('The Worker').

1615 Sheikh Ahmed Faruqi of Afghanistan.

1632 Shaikh-Pir Shattari.

1670 Yunus son of Adam.

18th century

1719 Murad Shami.

1750 Sheikh Mohamed Jamaludin of Adrianople, founded Jamalia Order.

1765 Salim Abdali.

1790 Pir-i-Do-Sara, Sarmouni.

19th century

1813 Mohammed Asghar.

1818 Sayed Sabir Ali-Shah.

1832 Sheikh Qalandar Shah, Suhrawardi.

1846 Sheikh Nasir el-Din Shah.

1854 Sayed Shah, Qadiri.

1860 Sayed Imam Ali Shah.

APPENDIX

1864   Sayed Mohamed Shah (Jan-Fishan Khan).

1870   Awad Afifi, the Tunisian.

1881   Sayed Ghaus Ali Shah.

20th century

1900   Dervish Bahaudin Ankabut of Bokhara.

1962   Sufi Abdul-Hamid Khan of Qandahar.

1965   Sheikh Daud of Qandahar.